The Mishpucah

Growing Up Jewish in Early Palo Alto

By
Louise Henriques Mann
As told to her daughter: Susie Washington Smyth

The Mishpucah

National Library of Canada Cataloguing in Publication Data
Henriques Mann, Louise, 1909-
The mishpucah : growing up Jewish in early Palo Alto / by Louise
Henriques Mann, as told to her daughter, Susie Washington Smyth.

ISBN 0-9733752-0-5

1. Jews—California—Palo Alto—Biography. 2. Levin family. 3. Palo
Alto (Calif.)—Biography. I. Washington Smyth, Susie, 1942- II. Title.

F869.P2H46 2003 979.4'73004924 C2003-911260-8

Grateful acknowledgement is made to the Palo Alto Historical Association for the use of their photos.

Book design and layout: Desktop Publishing Ltd., Victoria BC desktoppublishing@shaw.ca
Printed in Canada

Cover photo:
Palo Alto Tree, 1900, Palo Alto Historical Association.
Julia and Jacob Levin's family, 1916

Title:
Mishpucah is Yiddish for the extended family – parents, grandparents, siblings, uncles, aunts, cousins (first, second, once removed) – all form part of the extended family Jews call mishpucah.

Dedication

I am writing my memoirs for my children, grandchildren, and future generations so they will know something of their background. I regret that some of our early history is incomplete and I hope that others in my family, and dear family friends, will add their memories to this story so that there will be a more complete record of the Levin family.

There are many stories to tell. Unfortunately, I can only recall some of them and cannot verify the accuracy of some of the events that took place. For example, our story starts only with what my cousin, Gerry Marcus, and I can remember because all the records of our extended family have been lost. Because so many of my sisters, brothers and cousins are gone, and I am now in my 94th year, I realized that if I didn't record our family history, at least through to my mother's death, it too would be lost. That being said, I have asked my extended family (those still living) if they could share any important events that I had overlooked. I thank them for their help and, with that, I leave all further story telling to future generations.

I also want to thank all the family and friends who have helped in the publication of this book. Two deserve to be singled out. This book would have never been published if my favorite son-in law, Ian, had not pushed me to record my memories and my daughter, Susie, had not spent many hours transcribing and organizing my stories into a chronological format as well as a readable tale. However, all errors or omissions are mine.

I dedicate this book to Julia Levin, my mother. She was one of the most remarkable women I have ever known. She was loved and respected by all who knew her, and she was devotedly called Mama by practically everyone.

Louise L. Henriques Mann

Foreword

This book is rooted in our family. It focuses on the lives of my grandparents, and describes what life was like for my mother and her sisters and brothers, growing up in early Palo Alto, California. Unfortunately, the story only touches on our extended family and is hardly a complete family history. Yet, whenever I read these pages I am reminded of the love and affection of my relatives, whose lives are co-mingled here in Julia and Jacob Levin's story.

My mother, Louise, is a great storyteller and has provided almost all of the stories and the recipes in the book, with help from her sister Dorie, her brother Syd, Cousin Stanley and Gerry Marcus. I have tried to put their stories in chronological order and to develop them in ways that remain respectful of the living while being true to the family history.

It turns out that storytelling is a family trait. My grandfather, whom I never knew, loved to laugh and pass along a good story or dirty joke as he made his rounds with his horse and wagon, and later his truck. My grandmother also loved a good story. Together, they must have passed along the love of a good tale to their children.

I am especially grateful to my husband, Ian, for his love and support, for it is he who encouraged Mom to start telling her tales. Cousin Jeanne Louise edited the first part of the book and on several occasions, our friend Patrick Nagle reviewed the draft, which, believe me, was essential to help re-weave the remnants of our family's history. My inherited and loving daughter Cynthia copy-edited much of this book, updated Grandma's recipes and continuously encouraged me, especially when I got frustrated. Cousin Stan has provided the family tree in the Appendix to this book, which will help the reader understand who married who, and begat whom. Many cousins provided the photos of family members. Steven Staiger, Historian of the Palo Alto Historical Association, deserves special mention. He permitted us to reprint many of the old photos from early Palo Alto, and also reviewed the chapters on old Palo Alto for accuracy.

The most important thing I have learned as I have transcribed our family stories is that one's life almost always builds on the values and the many lessons we learn at our mother's and grandmother's knee. My hope is that, in this story, readers will find the shared Levin Family belief that we can continue to build strong families and healthy children, ready to act on a deep sense of service to our communities.

So, as Grandma would say, "Come in mein kinder, have something to eat and let me tell you the news."

Susie Washington Smyth

Contents

Ellis' and Jacob's Family

Things aren't what they used to be, which is often a reason to be thankful. In the 21st century, families can easily move, and have the opportunity to live all over the world. We think nothing of international travel: we walk on an airplane and, hours later, emerge on another continent. We communicate daily with each other by phone, email and television. Globally, we often share the same news at the same time. In the 19th and early 20th centuries, life was quite different. News was in

Jacob Levin around age 1 (Papa was always good looking)

print, people communicated by letter, families lived close to each other, record-keeping was done by hand, and family histories were, for the most part, oral.

For Russian Jews, record-keeping has been even more difficult. Between the willful brutality of the Czar and the genocides carried out by the Nazis and Stalin, life was never certain. As a result, the Levin family's oral record extends only as far back as my father's grandfather, whose name (we think) was David Levi. Family estimates are that he must have been born around 1820. We don't know his wife's name, but we do know that one of his children, Solomon Levi, or Shlomo Levi as he was probably called, was born in the 1840s.

Solomon married Deborah Barkusky, and they were said to have had 12 children, although only two of them lived beyond the age of 21. One of them was Uncle Ellis (or Elias, as he was named) who was born in 1868, just three years after the American Civil War ended. The other was my father, Jacob, who was born in 1878. To put that

Jacob's Bar Mitzvah photo, with parents

in a historical context, this was just two years after the last of the big Indian Wars—the Battle of Little Big Horn, Custer's Last Stand.

Solomon's occupation is unknown. No one remembers where he lived, but it is likely that it was in a shtetl (a Jewish village) not far from Vilna, which was the center of Jewish culture. Vilna originally was in Lithuania, but when the country was conquered by Russia in 1795, along with Poland, the Ukraine and part of Galicia, our ancestors became subjects of the Czar of Russia.

The Levin family must have lived within the Pale of Settlement, which in 1795 had been created by Russia to contain the large Jewish population of central Europe. At that time, Jews could not own land or become professionals; they could only engage in a limited number of occupations such as peddling, small shops, working on farms, and in various handicrafts such as sewing and carpentry. While we don't know Grandfather Solomon's occupation, we do know that Ellis was trained to be a cabinet maker and my father, Jacob, an upholsterer. Some in the family believe that Solomon was probably a carpenter, although Mama once said that he was a tailor. Mama also told me that, even though Solomon and his wife were very poor, they were always loving and wonderful to her. She remembered Solomon as a very tall and distinguished man.

Times were not easy for Jews in Russia. Prior to the reign of Nicholas I (1825-1855), the treatment of Jews alternated between extreme repression and abuse, and periods of relaxed restrictions. Under Nicholas I conditions deteriorated: his aim was the destruction of the Jewish community as a social and religious body. Then, under his successor, Alexander II (1855-1881), conditions substantially improved, and, for a time, Jews dared to hope to win equal rights as citizens.

However, in 1881, Alexander II was assassinated and his successor, Alexander III, pursued a rigorous anti-Jewish policy. Almost immediately, there was a wave of pogroms, followed by the imposition of severely repressive regulations, including the conscription of young male Jews under the age of 25 for service in the army.

Beginning in 1882, more than two million Jews left the Pale, mainly emigrating to the United States. My Uncle Ellis, who was 10 years older than Papa, became a part of this exodus in the late 1880s. He landed at Ellis Island in New York, and almost immediately went to Chicago. He lived on the West Side (the center of a burgeoning population of Central European Jews) where he had some family and friends from his life in Lithuania. In Chicago, Uncle Ellis found a job as a carpenter, working for the Karpen Brothers, Jewish owners of a large furniture factory, and immediately started learning English. He filed a declaration of his intention to become a citizen in 1890, and achieved that goal in 1893, the earliest possible date he could be granted citizenship.

Recently, the online Ellis Island Archive has offered a database for people tracking family members who entered the United States there. We have attempted to find the records or the dates for when Ellis or Jacob entered the United States, but have been unsuccessful. The archival records of the website are incomplete, and the names, given to immigrants as they entered or written down in the records, are not necessarily their family names. Thus, we are still uncertain about the entry dates and associated records for both Ellis and Jacob.

We do know that, in 1891, their aunt, Hannah Barkusky Kozoll, the oldest sister of his mother, and widow of Chaim Kozoll, arranged for their first cousin, Tsipa (Anne) Barkusky to emigrate from Vilna. Not surprisingly, as a widow with five small children Hannah was extremely poor. Thus, Anne, at age 16, was the only child of this branch of the family to emigrate to North America, where she married Ellis. It was not uncommon for cousins to marry each other at that time, nor was it uncommon to have arranged marriages.

So, in Chicago, began the start of the Levin family in America. Ellis and Anne married shortly after Anne's arrival there, and their three oldest children were born there: Dora, Gertrude Katherine (Katy) and Sarah. In 1898, they moved to Phoenix, Arizona, because it was feared that Ellis had contracted consumption (which we now call tuberculosis), an illness common among Central European Jewry in the United States. After spending only six months in Phoenix, first living in a tent and then in a clapboard house, they moved to San Francisco. Unable to find work there as a carpenter, Ellis borrowed a horse and wagon, and became a junk man. Initially he traveled the streets of San Francisco with his horse and wagon, picking up and reselling miscellaneous or discarded goods, such as rags and burlap sacks. Very soon afterwards, the family moved to San Jose, where Ellis established his own junkyard on South First Street: it was called the San Jose Bottling Works. He sold cleaned bottles, rags, and some scrap metal at the junkyard. Shortly after arriving in San Jose, a son, given the anglicized name of Henry, was named after his maternal grandfather, Chaim Kozoll, and another daughter, Bertha (who we called Bobby), were born.

Another aunt of my Uncle Ellis and of my father, Jacob, was Feive, who had two children, Samuel and Pauline. Pauline Barkusky also emigrated to the United States, and married Louis Barrish whose family also came from Russia. They married in San Francisco and had two children, Jack and Ruth. Pauline died fairly young from cancer. Quite a few years later, Louis Barrish· married Dora Edelstein Singer (my mother's step sister), who had been living in Chicago. There is more about Dora and Louis Barrish in later chapters.

Anne and Ellis Levin with children: Dora, Katy, Sarah and Henry

As for the children of Ellis and Anne, Dora, the eldest daughter, married Sam Edelstein, Mama's half brother. (There is more about this branch of the family in the chapter on Julia's family.) Katy married at least four times over her life, but had no children. Sarah married Isidor Marcus, who was a furrier, and they had two children, Audre and Gerald (Gerry), of whom more will be said in later chapters. Henry married four times and had five children: Ronald, Mary Anne, Robert (Bob), Michael and Ilene, Bertha, whom we called Bobby, married Craig Taylor, a professor at UCLA—they had no children.

Pauline Barrish

Louis Barrish with children, Jack and Ruth

The Family of Ellis and Anne Levin

Dora Levin Edelstein

Katherine (Katy) Levin (she was always exotic looking)

Henry Levin

Sarah Levin Marcus and Isidor Marcus with children: Audre and Gerry

Bertha (Bobbie) Levin Taylor, (young and mischievous)

Henry's children: Robert Levin, Ronal Vogel, Ilene Levin Hames, Michael Levin

Anne and Ellis' 50ᵗʰ Wedding Anniversary: Bobby, Katy, Henry, Sarah, Dora are standing

To close the loop on Ellis' and Jacob's family, the brothers had a warm and close personal relationship, even though they had been separated for many years and had a 10-year age difference between them. As a result, when Papa emigrated to the United States in October 1903, he took the unusual step of bypassing New York and Chicago (the destinations of choice for most Eastern European Jews), and instead went directly to San Jose where he joined Ellis in business.

If you're not already confused by all the family marriages, offspring and connections described in this chapter you almost certainly will be after the next chapter. Readers are encouraged to refer to the Levin Family Tree, found in the Appendix to this book.

Papa's passport, Vilna 1903: He used his mother's maiden name on his passport

(Most of the information contained in this chapter was provided by Gerry Marcus.)

Julia's Family

Unfortunately, as with so many Russian Jewish immigrants, the records of both my parents' families are lost. (We looked on several websites to see if we could find family records, but were unsuccessful). Therefore my mother's family history is recorded from my memory, and extends back only two generations.

Julia (Dickenfadden Edelstein) Levin, age 3 (Mama)

My grandmother's name was Esther Lustenik. She married Isadore Dickenfadden, but we know that this was not his real name. Rather, it was one he assumed so that there would be no written record of his real family name, because he had a younger brother and did not want him to be conscripted into the army. My mother, Julia, was born in Moscow on March 14, 1884, approximately one year after my grandparents' marriage. Mama was always very proud of her birthplace, and told us she came from an educated family—not born in the shtetl like most Jewish citizens in Russia at that time.

Mama's father was a violinist in the Czar's army. Mama used to say he was a concert violinist, but because her father died when she was just over a year old, her stories about him are based on hearsay. Mama said that my grandfather died of pneumonia when he was about 25 years old—a legacy of the harsh conditions he had experienced in the army, which permanently damaged his health and left him ill-prepared for the severe Moscow winters. It is important to remember that homes

Lustenik/Edelstein family in Russia: Aunt Lipka is seated on left, my grandmother Esther is next to her. Harry, Joseph and Lena Edelstein are on the right.

in Russia at that time did not have any insulation, nor were there sewage systems or natural gas distribution systems for heat. As a result, it was not uncommon for many people in Russia to die quite young.

My grandmother had two older sisters: Aunt Lipka, of whom more will be said later, and one (whose name we don't know) who married Joseph Edelstein, a tailor from Kiev. They had a son, Harry, and a daughter, Lena. Shortly after giving birth to Lena, my grandmother's sister died. In Russia, amongst the Jewish people, it was the custom of a widow or a widower to marry a relation of the deceased person. Thus, after the death of her sister, my grandmother, Esther, married Joseph Edelstein. As a result of that marriage, Mama's first cousins, Henry and Lena, became her step

Joseph & Esther Edelstein, with Nathan, Harry, Lena and Julia

brother and her step sister. In a family photo, Mama and Lena are dressed alike, so they must have been very close in age.

Mama said that she and her mother moved to Kiev with Joseph and his family after the marriage Although the Jews in Russia were constantly harassed, and limited in the type of work they could do, Joseph was reported to be a very fine tailor who made clothing for the officers of the Czar's army. Mama said that Joseph was a very kind and gentle man, and treated her as one of his own children. After marrying Joseph, my grandmother Esther bore him three sons: Nathan, Jack, and Samuel (Sam) Edelstein.

Mama was about 10 years old when my grandmother, who must have been around 32 years old, died from cholera. Poor Joseph was a widower again, this time with the respon-

Julia, age 8 or 9

sibility of six children. Looking for a better life, he decided to emigrate to America with his four sons (Harry, Nathan, Samuel and Jack). Mama was left in Russia with her mother's remaining sister, Aunt Lipka. I don't know who cared for Lena. After arriving in the United States, Joseph moved from New York to Connecticut and married two more times. He divorced the first U.S. wife shortly after the marriage. His second wife in the United States gave birth to yet another child, a daughter, Dora Edelstein. This wife took off shortly after her daughter was born, and left Joseph and his sons to take care of Dora. After this, Joseph and his family moved to Chicago.

Henry (Harry) Edelstein Singer in U.S. Navy

Henry, the eldest son, was thirteen or fourteen when the males of the family emigrated to the United States. Shortly after arriving, Henry decided to enlist in the Navy. Because he was under age, Henry lied about his age in order to get inducted, but the Navy soon found out and he was immediately rejected. Shortly thereafter, and knowing what to expect, Henry re-enlisted and this time, when asked for his name, he looked across the street and saw a sign advertising Singer Sewing Machines. Looking back at the recruiter, he said, "Singer." From that time on, Henry and his branch of family adopted the name Singer.

Henry, while in the Navy, fought in the Spanish American War, under the command of Teddy Roosevelt. After serving his term in the Navy, he moved to Minneapolis, Minnesota, married and had two children, Richard and Edith. Eventually Henry and his family moved to California. Edith married Hy Goldman in San Francisco in the 1930s (they are both deceased) and had two children, Paul and Linda, who live in California. Henry's grandson, Paul Goldman, recently told me that he still has his grandfather's war medals.

From my perspective, there is an interesting postscript to this branch of the family. It was at Edith's wedding that I first met my future husband, Fred Henriques—he bowed, clicked his heels and kissed my hand. I could hardly believe his colonial manners; quite different from those of my rough-and-ready brothers.

As for the rest of the sons, Nathan, the oldest from Joseph's second marriage, moved to St. Louis and married a woman named Sabrina. They had two sons, Joe (who was named after his grandfather), and Jack Edelstein. Joe became a pharmacist, and when he was going to university worked for my sister Dorie's husband, Ted Smolen. Joe still lives in the San Francisco Bay Area. Nathan's other son, Jack, died many years ago.

In his later years, Nathan moved to the Bay Area, and he worked in the Fun House at the San Francisco Amusement Park out at Ocean Beach. This was where the famous Laughing Lady graced the front entrance of the Fun House for years, until the amusement park was demolished. I think somebody in San Francisco bought the Lady, and I hope she is still laughing somewhere today. Uncle Nathan, who was a bit of a jokester, was in charge of the Spinner at the Fun House as part of his duties. The spinner was a flat disk that spun with centrifugal force and, unless you sat in the middle, everyone who rode it was bounced off to the sides of the room. Another job that Nathan enjoyed was to push air though holes in the floor when pretty girls came through the door, to blow their skirts over their heads. I think there were accompanying sound effects, and I am certain Nathan caught a naughty look each and every time a good-looking woman passed through the Fun House!

Nathan and Sabrina Edelstein with children: Jack and Joe

Louise and Uncle Jack Edelstein

My children, and especially those of my sister Jeannette, have fond memories of the Amusement Park because their Great Uncle Nathan would give them free tickets to ride the roller coaster that gave a great view of the Pacific Ocean. I expect he showed additional sights to my nephews, Bob and Joe.

Nathan's younger brother, Jack Edelstein, married and lived in Chicago for the early part of his adult life. He had two sons and a daughter. Bob, the eldest, became a dentist. Joe became a stockbroker, and was the person who encouraged me in the early 1960s, after my husband Fred died, to become a stockbroker. In fact, I worked for Joe when he was the vice-president of York and Company in Menlo Park.

Sadly, Jack's daughter was run over by a streetcar in Chicago and, shortly after, his wife died of tuberculosis. Not surprisingly, he came to California to be with his family, and brought his two boys. Jack married a second time to a woman who also had two children. Eventually, Jack and his younger brother, Sam Edelstein, started the Service Printing Company, of which more will be said later.

Sam, the youngest brother, was a quite a philanderer and playboy. As a young man, Sam joined the Navy and, for a time, he too used the surname Singer. I believe he traveled worldwide. At some point he was stationed in Japan and, of interest to my brothers, got a tattoo of a Japanese lady on his upper arm (she was dressed). In his later years, Sam would impress the younger members of our family by making the lady dance by flexing his arm muscles.

Eventually, Sam also moved to California and changed his name back to Edelstein. In California, Sam started in sales as a shoe salesman. In due course, he married Dora Levin, the eldest daughter of Ellis and Anne (Papa's older brother and sister-in-law). Mama acted as "match maker" for the two, and came to rue her role in this marriage because of Sam's behavior. Sam and Dora had two children, Harold and Jerome. When we were young kids and lived on Emerson Street, they lived around the corner from us on Addison. Because they were all about the same age, Harold and Jerome played a lot with my younger brother Richard, my cousin Gerry Marcus, and my sisters Dorie and Jeanette.

I think when Sam married Dora, he was still a salesman. During the period of time they lived in Palo Alto, Sam decided that he would start up a junk business and there was some talk of working with Papa. However, Sam liked to gamble in addition to his womanizing. Unfortunately, he lost his savings from gambling, so their family moved to San Francisco where he went to work as a shoe salesman for Somner and Kaufman. I'm sure he was good at sales because Sam always had a good story to tell

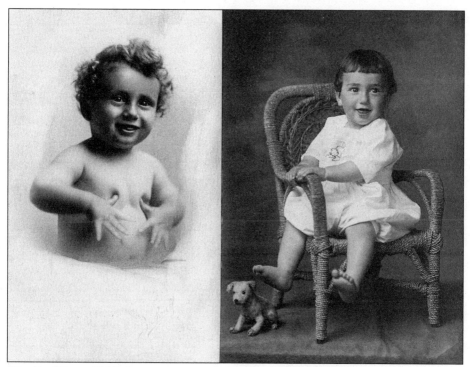

Harold and Jerome Edelstein

anyone who listened. In fact, when Sam eventually went into the printing business with his brother Jack, he was the salesman who got the accounts, and Jack ran the plant until he died of a heart attack. Subsequently, Sam took over the Service Printing Company until he sold it to his son Jerome, whose family still runs a very successful printing business today. Jerome printed the original Levin Family Cookbook produced by my sister Jeanette and her daughter Jeanne many years ago.

As for Lena, I believe the story went that she ran off with somebody, got married and moved to New York, although I don't know with whom, or when. We do know that Lena lived in New York because she met Mama upon her arrival in the United States (detailed more fully in another chapter). Unfortunately, we could find no record of when Lena entered the United States on the Ellis Island website. As a child, I remember that Mama occasionally would correspond with Lena when she could get somebody to scribe a letter in English for her, and I know that Sam Edelstein kept in touch with her when he was a young man. I also remember that when my sister Esther went to New York for the first time, she met Lena, but, unfortunately for the rest of us, Lena is lost in the mists of time, because nobody in the family remembers her married name.

Joseph Edelstein family in Chicago: Sam, Joseph, Jack and Dora

Dora Edelstein Singer, the last child from Joseph Edelstein's many marriages, was Mama's step sister. When Dora left Chicago as a young woman to see her brother, Henry (now Harry) Singer, in Minneapolis, she changed her name to Dora Singer. Then, following a visit to our family in California, she decided to move west. Although we had no blood relationship, we were all very close to her; she was a remarkable person with fine character and a great sense of humor. Louis (Louie) Barish (see the chapter on Papa's family) met Dora shortly after she came west and he immediately became smitten. Louie had been a widower for some time, and was troubled that he was unable to properly care for his two children, Jack and Ruth (both of whom are now deceased). Well, Louie courted her quite seriously for some time and, although Dora hesitated, she eventually married him. Ruth just adored Dora, as we all did.

One of my favorite memories is the 1933 trip that Dora and I took to see the World's Fair, and also to visit family and friends in Chicago. We drove my 1929 Essex there, mostly on very poor roads, rented an apartment in Chicago for a week or so, and had a ball seeing the sights. When we got back from the trip, Dora and Louie conceived Paul, their only child. Dora was in her forties at the time she conceived, and I used to tease her that it was our trip that did it.

A few years later, Louie won a lottery of about three thousand dollars, and they bought a little dress shop in Redwood City that Dora ran. Paul, their son, joined the Navy around World War II became a career officer, and eventually retired to Carmel and subsequently moved to Cambria where he lives with his wife, Carole. They have many children and grandchildren, and their clan is always up for a family gathering.

There is an interesting postscript to Louis and Dora. When they aged and moved to the Jewish Home in San Francisco, and after Louis died, Dora—ever adventurous even in her old age—had a second romance, and married an older man also living in the home. She died in her 90s, and her second husband was very devoted to her until the end.

Louis and Dora (Edelstein Singer) Barrish, 1956

Aunt Lipka

No story about Mama would be complete without saying something about Aunt Lipka. She was Mama's maiden aunt (an older sister to my grandmother Esther), who was very loving to my mother and helped raise her after my grandmother died. I am named after her but, fortunately, my mother decided to anglicize the name and called me Louise instead.

Notwithstanding a lifelong problem with her back, Aunt Lipka was a very enterprising dress designer, Mama always said. She must have been a good designer and seamstress, because she traveled with an opera company that kept her moving about the country. And a good thing, too, because in those days, the person in charge of the wardrobe owned the costumes, as well as being responsible for keeping them in good repair.

From time to time, Aunt Lipka had to leave Mama in the care of someone when she traveled with the opera company. Other times she took Mama with her. I can remember Mama telling me she traveled to many wonderful places in Russia. She had been in St Petersburg, Kiev, Odessa, Minsk, Krakow (now in Poland) and various other big cities in Russia. When Mama traveled with Aunt Lipka, she saw the extreme poverty and misery among the Russian people, although they themselves traveled very comfortably. In fact, she told me that some of the aristocrats were so sorry for the poor people that they openly advocated revolt long before Lenin. Mama always said conditions in Russia were heartbreaking, and it certainly left a lasting impression on her, both physically, and also in ensuring that her family and friends always had enough to eat. She told me that it was not uncommon for people to actually starve in those days.

When Aunt Lipka could not take Mama with her on her travels, she would leave her both well provided for and well clothed. When she returned from her trip, she would always find Mama with very few clothes and often barefoot. Mama always would find somebody more needy than herself and gave food, shoes, clothes—even her overcoat—to them. This generosity was to be a hallmark of her life and is what I remember most about her. She always believed she had something she could share with others less fortunate. And, believe me, she taught us by example. As kids, I remember that we girls always said to each other that we wanted to be half as generous and loving as Mama.

Mama was taught to crochet and sew by Aunt Lipka, as most girls were taught at that time, but she also had some schooling. She could read Russian, Yiddish and Hebrew. This was somewhat unusual because most girls in Czarist Russia received no education at all. I remember that, when we were kids, Mama subscribed to the *Jewish Forward*. It was written in Yiddish, so we kids couldn't read it, but she sure loved reading the news. I think the *Jewish Forward* was a socialist paper, and I know Mama would have made a good socialist, given her beliefs. Indeed, she often would speak with disgust about the "Respublicans" (a variation on the Russian word for Republic), their selfishness, their need for great personal wealth, and their lack of care for those less fortunate.

I don't remember what happened to Aunt Lipka, but she must have died when Mama was in her teens because it was then when Mama moved from Moscow to work in a cigarette factory in Vilna, where they custom-made cigarettes for aristocrats. I think that is where she got her lifelong intense dislike of tobacco. Mama sure made life miserable for anyone who smoked. She claimed she could not breathe with cigarette smoke in the air—as usual, way ahead of her time.

Julia Meets Jacob

When Mama was 18 and living in Vilna, the story goes that she was walking with a friend in a park, and that this was the day she met Papa. Papa was 24, and he too was in the park with a bunch of guys, all of whom were showing off, trying to pick up the two girls. Papa always liked to show off his strength: this time he was demonstrating how high he could swing, in order to get the attention of the two girls. Somehow, he took a dive off the swing, and got a very bloody nose. Mama's friend and the boys all laughed at Papa, but Mama, with her great feeling for someone in distress, wet her handkerchief, bent over, and helped wipe his bleeding nose. Apparently, this caring, slim, very attractive 5'2" young lady with tight-curly, light-brown hair and smiling brown eyes so impressed Papa that he instantly made a date with her.

My father was very tall for men at that time—nearly six feet—and strikingly handsome. He had jet-black hair, fair skin and beautiful smiling eyes. He was a great storyteller, and the many stories about him suggest that he must have been quite a ladies' man. In any event, they soon fell in love. Mama, also had another, slightly older, suitor who had money, and was very serious about courting Mama. He bought her candy and other gifts, which Papa would eat when he called on Mama. One time, when Papa and Mama were taking a walk, they saw a lady selling violets and she said, "I like violets." Papa said, "I like violets too," but he didn't buy her any. Oh well, they were in love, and they ended up deciding that they would get married.

Because Mama was an orphan, and without close relatives in Russia, she had no money, except what she earned at the cigarette factory. In Europe at the turn of the twentieth century, both Jewish and Christian girls were not considered a "good match" without a dowry. Yet Papa married Mama without a dowry, and also paid for the whole wedding. Mama always said they had an extravagant wedding and that everything was "first class". Mama arrived at the wedding in a carriage, and although

Mama, possibly her wedding photo

Papa seated on the left, with his friends: wedding photo

Julia, Jacob and baby Esther

there are two photos of Mama taken around that time, I am unable to verify which is the wedding photo of her. There is also a photo of Papa with his friends from the upholstery factory, that I presume was taken at the wedding, based on the way everyone was dressed.

At the time of their marriage, Papa was living with his folks, Solomon Levi and Deborah Barkusky. His family was poor, and they needed the extra financial help Papa provided because his older brother, Ellis, had already moved to America. However, when Mama and Papa got married, they moved to their own little house, near his family in Vilna. Esther, their first child, was born on March 14, 1902, on Mama's nineteenth birthday.

While my parents were happy, they lived in a time of persecution against the Jews and of the excesses of the rich. These occurred while people of all faiths were starving, especially the rural peasants. As children, we always heard Mama say, "Eat, mein kinder, there is food." The bounty of California must have been a constant reminder to my parents of those hungry years in Russia, when there was little to eat other than cabbages and potatoes, with an occasional soup-bone for meat flavor.

Mama once told me that they dug holes in their backyard and stored the cabbages and potatoes in the ground, because Russia was so cold in the winter that everything froze. Storing these vegetables in the ground prevented them from freezing and kept them chilled and fresh. Of course, food that is plentiful now, and easy to take for granted, like bananas from South America, mandarin oranges from China, exotic cheeses from France, or pineapples from Hawaii, was simply not available to the average person at the beginning of the twentieth century in Russia, and apparently is not, even to this day. Even with these slim pickings, Mama was a fantastic cook, and with the short winter days, Mama's cabbage soup must have been very welcome.

*****

Mama's Russian Borscht

10 cents of cracked soup bone (substitute 1-2 pounds short ribs)
2 quarts water
1 large onion, chopped
1 large potato, diced (optional)
2 cloves garlic
1 large can diced tomatoes
salt and pepper to taste
½ head of cabbage, finely sliced
2 tablespoons brown sugar
juice of 1 lemon

In a large pot, bring the water and meat to a boil, skimming and simmering, covered, for one hour. Add onion, potato, garlic, tomatoes, salt and pepper to taste. Simmer for another hour. Add the cabbage, sugar and lemon juice. Correct the seasoning. Serve when cabbage is tender.

*****

Shortly after Esther was born, Papa was at a park, listening to some people speak out against the Czar and the government. The Cossacks suddenly arrived on horseback and they attacked and whipped everyone in the park, killing many people. Papa was just able to escape. He had welts all over him and, to make matters worse, the Cossacks came, door to door, looking for anyone who had welts or disfigurations, so they could arrest and kill them. Mama must have known they were coming, so she hid Papa in the basement in the coal chute, and when they searched the house, they couldn't find him.

This episode, combined with the pogroms and the constant discrimination against the Jewish people, helped Mama and Papa decide to leave Russia. Because Uncle Ellis was already established in the United States, and the brothers had a close relationship, Papa and Mama decided that their future would be to come to the land of opportunity—America.

One story is that, in early 1903, Papa walked out of Russia to hide from the Czar's army and Cossacks. If he did so, it must have been an extremely difficult journey. We do know that, at some point in his travels, he took the train to Germany and from there, he came across, steerage class, on a ship and entered the United States at Ellis Island in 1903. From there, he went directly to San Jose.

After Papa left Vilna, Mama moved in with her in-laws because they only had enough money saved for one passage. But there was a surprise – soon after Papa left, Mama realized that she was pregnant again. Elaine, their second daughter, was born January 1, 1904.

In speaking of her life with Papa's family, Mama had only praise for her in-laws and their love for her and their two grandchildren. Once in the United States, Mama and Papa regularly kept in touch with his parents and, of course, wrote to them in Russian. As a young child, I can remember Mama sending them clothes and food packages. I think my parents lost touch with them just after World War I, during the Russian Revolution. We presumed they must have been killed, and had no way of finding them because of the sheer numbers of displaced people in Russia at that time.

By late 1904, Papa had saved enough money for Mama to come to the States. Over the winter, she packed what little belongings she had—including the brass candlesticks that had belonged to her mother (they are now with my niece, Jeanne Louise), a few pieces of jewelry, and a samovar (which my niece, Joan Fox, has refinished). She bundled up Esther and Elaine, and left Russia on March 23, 1905, for the United States. It must have been heartbreaking for Solomon Levi and Deborah Barkusky because they knew they would never see their grandchildren again.

Mama's passport, Vilna, 1905: She used Jacob's mother's maiden name

Note: The family name of Mama's passport was Papa's mother's maiden name. This was not an uncommon practice for immigrants arriving in the United States at the beginning of the twentieth century. We searched the Ellis Island website to see if we could find the entry date of Julia, Esther and Elaine into the United States, and who met them on arrival, but unfortunately we were unable to find any record, even using similar names.

Starting Out In America

Julia's Trip to the United States

Julia, Esther and Elaine in Russia: Just before leaving

In 1905, when Elaine was just a year old, and Esther was just three years old, Mama and her two young daughters began the difficult journey across the Atlantic to New York. Mama said that they first went to Germany where they boarded a ship for New York. The sea voyage may have taken 10 days or more, and the weather was stormy. Since Mama could get sick on a ferry boat, it is difficult to imagine how she managed with a three-year-old child and a nursing baby, traveling steerage class (the cheapest sleeping accommodation) all the way to the United States, and not able to speak a word of English! Plus, as my sister Jeanette recounted to her daughters, Mama had to pack enough food for the voyage because steerage class had no food service.

When Mama arrived in New York, her step-sister Lena met her at Ellis Island. Mama often laughed at herself when she told us that the first thing Lena did was to criticize her shoes and clothes, saying that she looked "old-fashioned" and "old country". At the very least, Lena insisted, "Buy new shoes." Mama had very little money to get to California, but she went shopping with Lena and spent most of her funds buying new shoes. My daughter, Susan, and granddaughter, Sierra, will tell you that Mama's need for new shoes is a family pattern, and that this trait is genetically endowed.

Within a week, Lena put Mama on the train going west. The train went by the southern route, which was safer because, in 1905, Indian uprisings were still occurring in Montana and also, it was the fastest way to go west. Mama said that on the trip through the southern United States, she saw her first black person. Still believing she would become rich beyond belief, and because at that time she was so fair (a trait attributed to the European rich who went to great lengths to keep out of the sun to show they did no manual work), she said to herself, "Mein dear, I'll be a princess."

Mama had no conception of the distance she would travel by train, and the story of the five-day trip across the United States was one of her favorites. She still was barely able to speak a word of English, and had her name and destination pinned on her coat. At first, all she and her children ate were bananas, because each time the train would stop at a station, vendors would go through the train with fresh fruit, and the only English word she knew for fruit was "pananas". Soon Mama realized she needed to get money for more food, and that just eating fruit was giving her children diarrhea.

Fortunately for Mama, there were drummers (traveling salesmen who went from town to town selling housewares) on the train, and one of them, who spoke Yiddish, helped Mama to pawn most of her jewelry to get food for the trip. However, by this time, both children had dysentery, and while Mama now had money for food, she only had enough money for a coach seat. Thus, she sat up all the way from New York to San Jose, holding a chamber pot on her lap for each child. In addition, she had to breast-feed baby Elaine on the train while coping with her prickly-heat rash and constant crying. I can only image how difficult this must have been for Mama, because she was both fastidiously clean and a modest woman by nature. Needless to say, she was extremely relieved and very happy to see Papa when he met her at the train in San Jose.

Life in San Jose

When my Uncle Ellis settled in San Jose his junk business was located on First Street, in what is now downtown San Jose. Uncle Ellis bought old bottles, and washed and re-sold them. He probably also bought and sold anything else he could, too, which must surely qualify him as one of the first recyclers on the West Coast. Yet the best part was that the business was successful. Uncle and Auntie were soon able to buy a home that was a block away on Second Street, and although I can barely remember it, it had two stories, and an eating area in the back with an overhanging trellis. I do remember the outdoor eating area, because later on, when Mama's half brother, Sam Edelstein, married my eldest cousin Dora at her parents' home, all of us little kids had to eat outside.

Not surprisingly, on the day that Papa arrived in San Jose, his elder brother immediately told him, "Don't even look for work as an upholsterer. Become a peddler or a junk man, work hard, and you will make a good living." So Papa started working with Uncle Ellis in his business, the San Jose Bottling Works, and there was some talk of them becoming partners.

Papa's job in the business was to take the horse and wagon, and travel as far south as Salinas and Santa Cruz to buy burlap sacks and other things from the farmers. At that time, there were big cattle ranches all over California. (One I recall, in Santa Clara Valley, was called Miller and Lux—one of many huge ranges these people owned in California and Nevada). Papa said he frequently would stay overnight at these ranches before returning home to San Jose, because they were too far for a day trip by horse and wagon. California was still a pretty wild country in the early part of the twentieth century, and these large ranches, many of them initially secured by land grants issued from the Mexican government, played an important stabilizing role in the State.

Papa and Uncle really enjoyed each other's company, and so it was easy for them to work together. But the wives were another story. When Mama arrived in San Jose, Ellis's wife, Anne, was not very pleasant to her, and they never did become close, maybe because she was jealous of Mama, or saw her as an interloper. I do know that

Mama often said Annie was bossy to her when she first arrived in San Jose, and used to refer to Mama as "the greenhorn", which was a popular tag for new immigrants at that time. It probably didn't help that Mama could hardly speak any English and, up until that time, hadn't much experience in doing housework because, even though her family in Russia was considered poor, they could still get help for the home.

Mama always said Auntie was a superb cook, and would occasionally give Mama a recipe—but she would always see to it that there was something missing, so that Mama's efforts would be a flop. Gerry Marcus, Ellis's grandson and my second cousin, says his grandmother and Mama were just two very strong ladies: both were very warm and loving, and both were fabulous cooks, but obviously they didn't get along very well— and everybody knew it!

Anne Kozol Levin

During the time they lived in San Jose, Mama and Papa had a small home quite close to the junkyard, but even though it was a nice neighborhood, Mama had a difficult struggle adjusting to her new life. It didn't take her long at all to realize that the streets were not paved with gold, and that making ends meet was not easy. Life was completely different in America: the help that was cheap in Russia was unavailable in California, and the very small income Papa initially made hardly fed the family. Mama said that, in the first year, she often had raw knuckles from washing out clothing stains with lye, and rubbing the clothes on a scrub board in an old tin washtub and, of course, from keeping the small house and children clean. It is hard to imagine now, but Mama had one dress at that time (I think she said it cost $1.95) which she washed by hand and ironed every day. By the way, I suspect the shoes Mama bought in New York were not very useful for her new life in San Jose.

Life in San Jose was so unpleasant for Mama, that she and Papa decided that they would move away and go into business for themselves. Papa initially wanted to open up a junkyard in Redwood City because it had a port where ships would dock, and he thought it would be a good town to start such a business. Mama would not hear of it! She said, "I want my children to grow up in a nice town, a university town, where they'll meet educated people." She won the family debate, and Papa decided to open up the business in Palo Alto. In hindsight, Mama, as usual, was prescient. Education was always of central interest in Palo Alto and, until "Silicon Valley" became the economic driver it is today, Palo Alto's main business was education.

As for Papa, he moved to Palo Alto first, to get established before he moved his family because, shortly after arriving in San Jose, Mama was pregnant again.

Irving was born at home in San Jose on February 19, 1906, not long before the famous San Francisco earthquake. Later that year when they moved, Mama came by train to Palo Alto with her three children. Papa was working and was unable to meet her at the station. When she got off at Palo Alto, Dan Hickey, the constable (who also ran a cartage service), immediately spotted "the greenhorn" as Jake the Junkman's Russian wife, and took her in a horse-drawn jitney (something like a taxi today) down the unpaved streets of Palo Alto to the new home Papa had rented for them on the 900 block of High Street.

I know that Papa and Mama struggled very hard in those early years. Papa often worked long hours and, because he traveled the area by horse and wagon, buying and selling junk, he frequently didn't return home until late at night. Mama worked, too. There was no electricity, a cold water sink, and a wood stove for cooking and to heat water on. I know Mama would have liked to have had an opportunity for some education to properly learn English (she could still barely speak English by the time my older sister Esther started school) but she, like Papa, had lots of chores and three young children to clothe and feed.

The Early Years In Palo Alto

To better understand our life as a family, it is important to know a bit about early Palo Alto, beginning with its name which, in Spanish, means "big stick". The town was named for the giant redwood tree that once stood by the railroad tracks near what is now the town line between Menlo Park and Palo Alto, across the street from the Stanford campus.

In the early part of the twentieth century, the Palo Alto I grew up in still retained a rural aspect. Orchards, hay fields and market gardens could still be found within walking distance of the town. In the spring, most of the Stanford campus was a carpet of poppies and wild lupin. The town itself was quite small, with a few side streets, and one main street that went directly into Stanford. The street was aptly named University Avenue.

In addition to its redwoods, the town was best known for its beautiful oak trees in the middle of the streets that stayed unpaved until many years later. The trees remained on the roads all during the time when there were horses. When cars came along, the city fathers ordered most of the trees to be cut

Palo Alto Redwood,1891
(Palo Alto Historical Association)

down because drivers, unlike horses, were always running into them. There was one particularly beautiful oak tree that was on University Avenue and Waverley Street—right in the middle of the sidewalk—and it was the place to meet, and to be seen. It was called The Decker Oak, and was beautiful and green most of the year. It finally died and was cut down in 1924.

Decker Oak: The Place to Meet—Corner of University and Waverley (Palo Alto Historical Association)

During the first two decades of the 1900s, what is now Palo Alto was mostly hay farms because the climate was so ideal for hay. I read once that some of the hay was shipped to San Francisco for the city's fire-department horses because of its high quality. There were also farms that raised produce, and many that had fruit trees of all kinds within walking distance of the original town site. One I remember very well: it was across the street from the public swimming pool, located on Embarcadero Road, across what is now Newell Road. (The pool was a small circle, shallow on the sides and deep in the middle.) In those days, a farmer raised tomatoes there—big, beautiful, beefsteak tomatoes—as well as other kinds of produce. As kids, when we went swimming, every once in a while we'd scarf a couple of tomatoes. They tasted so good after a swim. We knew we were in the wrong, but fortunately we never got caught.

Originally Palo Alto was established as a "dry" town. This was primarily because of the Stanford family's influence. Many people have always thought that it was because Mrs. Stanford was a teetotaler, but she was not. In fact, the Stanford family were the largest grape growers in California at the time. However, Senator and Mrs. Stanford insisted that the University, dedicated to their son, must be free of alcohol—it was a politically correct position at the time. As a result, Senator Leland Stanford required that Palo Alto, if it was to serve as a center for University business and be connected by road to the University, must be clean (dry) too. To ensure this requirement was enforced, Timothy Hopkins (a longtime associate of Stanford in the railroad business), who had established the original town's boundaries on adjacent lands from his family's estate, placed a covenant on the deed for the town site, ensuring that no liquor could be sold within the town's original boundaries. That meant no liquor could be sold in Palo Alto within one mile of the Stanford campus—a prohibition that extended well into the 1970s.

Mayfield (the area that is now California Avenue and El Camino) was another story. It was an older, established community and a very free, swinging place. I was told by Papa that Senator Stanford had initially approached the Mayfield town fathers about building the University nearby—with his condition of no booze—but that he was refused because saloons were a big source of revenue for the town, there being 13 of them at the time. I believe Mayfield originally was established because of the lumber industry. Many lumbermen, construction and wood workers temporarily lived and worked there because of the large loading dock and railroad access to San Francisco and San Jose. They came to log the beautiful redwoods of what is now Woodside, to rebuild San Francisco after the fires in the 1850s and 1860s. By 1905, when Papa first arrived in Palo Alto, there was a well-established railroad station and loading dock at Mayfield where the logs and other supplies were shipped to the City.

It is a well-known fact that San Francisco sustained the worst of the 1906 earthquake, but Palo Alto and Stanford University were hit fairly hard by it, too. Several of the two-story buildings in town fell down, and the entrance gates to the University at the corner of Palm Drive and El Camino Real were completely destroyed. Although several buildings on the Stanford campus sustained minor damage, the Memorial Chapel was heavily damaged. Worse yet, the Stanfords had imported Italian artisans to create a stunning (just completed) mosaic on the front of the Chapel and it was extensively damaged. And, there was a circular setting of beautiful marble statues that were religious representations; these, too, were demolished and were never rebuilt.

During this time Palo Alto had electric streetcars within the town and a train which connected the town to nearby communities. Fortunately, the transportation system was not too heavily damaged by the earthquake, because it was used to

After the Earthquake

University and High St., Palo Alto

Stanford Chapel
(Palo Alto Historical Association)

rebuild the town and the university, and to send supplies to San Francisco. Before cars became so popular, most people walked, or else took the trolley or train, which were considered progressive innovations. Trolleys started at El Camino Real, and went down University Avenue to where Bayshore Highway is today. A branch line turned south at Waverley Street and went as far as Oregon Avenue. The streetcar barn was located on Hawthorne, near Alma Street. The trolley also went to Stanford University, crossing El Camino at Palm Avenue. It did a thriving business, but was quickly abandoned in 1932 when automobiles became popular. The San Francisco-San Jose Railway also offered services to Los Altos, Cupertino and Los Gatos.This commuter train service eventually was purchased by Southern Pacific, and is now operated by Caltrain.

Papa moved into this setting just before the big earthquake, to start his own business. He named it the Palo Alto Junkyard. He was very proud of his business and I can still remember the sign on the building, "Established in 1905". In the early part of the 1900s everything was salvaged, so the junk business was profitable—particularly for an immigrant who could barely read or write English. Papa often told us he went into the junk business because a man could work as long as his strength permitted and, most importantly, he was free. He also said, "It was a good way to feed many mouths, because everyone knows me."

A few years ago, Papa's words came back to me. In 1995, Alfred Werry (an early Palo Alto icon) died at the age of 106. Al was born six years before the town of Palo Alto was incorporated. He owned Werry Electric, a well-known business in Palo Alto. In his obituary, he is quoted as witnessing dramatic changes in the city's commercial life: "Folks didn't go out much for groceries. The grocer and butcher, the baker and the candlestick-maker used to call on us. Even the junk man used to go through town hollering, 'Rags, bottles and sacks' and we'd give him old clothes and any junk we had around." (*Palo Alto Times*, February 24, 1995). That junk man was Papa!

Upon moving to Palo Alto, Papa bought horses from the Palo Alto Stock Farm that was on the original site of Leland Stanford's stock farm before it became the University. Mr. Stanford raised racehorses and, after he died, the University continued to raise stock horses for extra income. That is why people still call Stanford "The Farm". In the early days, Papa depended on his horses to help him in the business, and took very good care of them. He often said that The Farm could always be counted upon to provide good stock.

In the early days of the Palo Alto Junkyard, Papa bought and hauled a lot of junk from Stanford University, particularly in the years just after the earthquake. Because the buildings on the University were hit quite hard, especially the beautiful new Memorial Chapel, Dad helped haul some of the broken statues away. He also had pieces of mosaic and other kinds of building remnants from the University. Many years later, my brother Richard resurrected some pieces of the original mosaic from the Memorial Chapel, and used them, along with some large stones from San Fransquito Creek, to build a magnificent rock fireplace at our ranch located just behind what is now the Stanford Golf Course.

After this initial bonanza of salvage from the earthquake, Papa regularly bought from all the local businesses in the area, and also from the big estates in Woodside and Atherton, such as those owned by Flood and Hopkins—these people had made a great deal of money when the trains pushed west in the late nineteenth century. Dad bought almost anything—rags, bottles, sacks, furniture, iron and metal. In fact, Papa was almost always away from the Yard finding the merchandise to resell, and it was Mama who would mind the store, and buy or sell the junk—whatever the customers wanted. That was how she learned her English.

As for our family life, Papa and Mama spent their first few years in the rented house in the 900 block of High Street, which was also the first site of the Palo Alto Junkyard. The folks rented the property from the Kimble family, whose daughter Alice befriended Mama in many ways, helping her to learn English and teaching Mama to sew clothes for the increasing number of children in the family. Alice married a man named Mr. Tyler, and they had two daughters—Betty, who went through school with me, and Marion, who was younger. Charles Tyler, their son, became a good friend of my younger brother Richard.

Alice Tyler was very understanding and loving to Mama, and they developed a wonderful friendship. In later years, Mrs. Tyler developed tuberculosis, which she had caught from her daughter, Betty. Because there were no antibiotics to treat this disease and it was contagious, Mr. Tyler built a small cabin for his wife and daughter, behind the garage on Bryant near Forrest. Mama, who really loved this woman, her first American friend, used to bring soup and food to her all the time. An interesting postscript to this story is that, in 1937, Fred and I moved into this cabin—it was our first home—just after we got married.

With Papa working long hours, the business started to grow, and so did Mama. David, their second son, was born February 9, 1908, at home on High Street. I was born seventeen months later, on September 14, 1909, shortly after we had moved to our new home on Homer Avenue. Mama always swore I was born on the 13th, and I celebrated that date until I got a copy of my birth certificate at the age of 28.

As for my brother David, his favorite story, and one that Mama also told, is how he refused to nurse when he was only nine months old. It turned out that Mama was pregnant with me and apparently Mama's milk didn't taste good any more. It sounds odd now because we know so much more medically, but in those days, there was a belief that a woman wouldn't get pregnant if she nursed, and generally Mama nursed us all for well over a year. However, in Mama's case, it didn't work. So my brother has always accused me of souring his milk! As for me, I have often wondered if that was why the first thing David looked at was a woman's breasts.

When I was a child, boy babies were more important than girls— Papa would always say he had four boys and

Levin family: Julia, Jacob Esther (Back Row) Elaine, Louise, David Irving (Front Row), 1910.

five children. I guess Mama cried after I was born, because she had wanted another son to please Papa. She must have been disappointed that I was another girl, and a homely one at that. She once told me that I looked like a monkey at birth. As the third daughter, I was destined to be named after Mama's Aunt Lipka. Fortunately for me, Mama had met Louise Owen, who lived next to the Tylers, so I assume she thought a good American name for me would be Louise instead of Lipka. (At the time I was born, families often named their children after a deceased relation.)

Mama said that my birth was difficult and they had to call a doctor. I was a blue baby—apparently it took a while for me to breathe. The doctor placed me in hot water, and then in cold. He even pierced my ear! Finally, I must have decided I'd better yell and cut out all this nonsense. Notwithstanding her initial disappointment, Mama loved me and we were very close. Some of my siblings have even accused me of having been Mama's pet.

Shortly after I was born, Mama developed a tapeworm. How she got it, I don't know, because she was so clean and insisted that we be clean as well. In fact, as we got older, it became a family joke when Papa took a bath, because we knew he was going to have sex with Mama. She insisted he be clean before becoming intimate and Dad didn't like bathing! As for the tapeworm, it must have been huge because Mama

Louise, age 2.

was devouring food constantly, and my older brothers told me that she wolfed down an entire loaf of bread at one time. Mama eventually got medicine to eliminate it. My two older brothers were so impressed by its size that they kept me entertained by telling stories about it when I was young. And I am sure the size of the tapeworm grew with each telling.

This reminds me that in all the hustle and bustle of our lives, there was always time for a good story. Dad was the all-time great storyteller. They were more often dirty stories, but he really could tell them and make people laugh. Papa must have enjoyed meeting the many different people in his travels, because he certainly had stories when he came home. We often would keep asking for yet another story until he told us, "Enough, go to bed!" I guess I inherited his ability to tell and appreciate a good joke.

On the other hand, Papa was cautious (you might say overly cautious), and often afraid to take a chance. Mama was the sharp trader who honed her skills at the junkyard, and was willing to take risks. She also was the organizer in the family, and was always and forever the optimist. To this day, I am certain that all of her children and grandchildren carry her realistic optimism within us, because there was room for no other option in our house!

Homer Avenue

Palo Alto was all that Mama had hoped for. Even the first streets in old Palo Alto, such as Homer, were named after writers and poets, which I suppose is the correct note for a university town. With my parents' enthusiasm for their newly adopted town, and as is with most young families, Papa and Mama soon became preoccupied with securing a home for their growing family. Around 1909, shortly before I was born, they had saved enough money to

Homer Avenue House

make a down-payment on their first house, which was at 561 Homer Avenue, near Webster Street. It was a very big decision for them. Getting a mortgage in those years was not as easy as it is today, and, having been born in Russia, they had no experience with the banking system.

Our house on Homer Avenue was on a lot 200 feet deep and about 50 feet wide. The house itself was a two-storied, brown shingled house. Shingled houses were popular in Palo Alto in the early part of the twentieth century and, well built, were often constructed out of redwood and oak. Our old house is still standing today, but has been significantly enlarged and remodeled since then, and moved to the back of the lot, formerly the site of the Palo Alto Junkyard.

When we lived on Homer Avenue, the house had a very small front-yard with no lawn, and low shrubs in front. As a young child, I thought the lot was very large, especially the back of the yard, which was where we had the stable for the horses and for the wagons. In the early part of the twentieth century most people did not have cars and we certainly couldn't afford one. However, Papa had three beautiful horses and two wagons. He used two horses on his long trips, and the third was a spare. While most of the back area was devoted to the junkyard, half the stable was used for storage, and Mama also kept chickens back there.

As a child, I remember that once the chickens stopped laying eggs, Papa would be called to come cut off their heads. I always watched, fascinated that the chicken's reflexes kept it jumping without its head. David did too. In fact, one time he reached for the chicken head just as Papa had cut it off. So did Dan the Dog. It was quite a fight, but Dan won, and David was badly scratched on his face. Well, Papa may have killed the chickens, but Mama always had the job of picking and drawing the chickens. Eventually, all of us girls had our share of these chores. I can still remember the smell of singed chicken feathers! Other times, Papa brought a baby goat home, which we would feed for about two weeks before Papa killed it. We kids never enjoyed goat meat because all we could visualize was the cute little kid, but our parents and Auntie and Uncle really enjoyed eating kid (baby goat).

When we lived on Homer, Papa occasionally would buy classic cars for salvage. Once he purchased a Franklin Steamer, and another time, a Stutz. They were impressive with wood interiors and plush, rolled upholstery, but I most vividly remember the day he came home with the carriage of Mrs. Stanford. It was the most gorgeous thing I had ever seen. My two older brothers and I had wonderful times playing in it before it was scrapped for junk. It had silver handles on it, and a vase for flowers. It is too bad we didn't keep it because, like so many other things that went through the yard, it would be a museum piece and worth a fortune today.

As for the house on Homer, when we lived there, it was small and had no electricity. We had a gas heater, and a few gaslights, and a gas meter that we had to feed with quarters to keep it going. I was about seven years old when we installed the first electricity in the house on Homer—one lightbulb in the kitchen and one bulb in the dining room. We thought this was modern living! Around this time, my parents put an ice box on the back porch, next to the wash tubs. Papa also kept a keg of beer on the back porch and would enjoy a glass or two every evening. Ever curious, David one day turned the handle on the spout to see what would happen, and because the beer was under pressure, he was unable to close it. The beer ran out flooding the back porch, and David got a strap from Papa for his efforts.

Mama cooked on a wood stove in the kitchen, and there might have been gas for hot water, although we also had hot water from the wood stove. There were two bedrooms upstairs, with no toilet nearby. Papa and Mama had one of the bedrooms with the youngest child. The rest of us slept in this other big room. In fact, I did not have my own room until I was 25 years old, and working in the bank. We children all shared a double bed with a sibling. When we were young, there were at least four to a room. As a young child, I never felt abandoned at bedtime because I always had company. However, all of us could hear everything anybody else said upstairs. I even remember hearing Mama getting mad at Papa, because at night he would fill the chamber pot to the brim and was too lazy to take it down, and so she would have to bring it downstairs in the morning! Generally, men never did a thing in the house—and Papa was no different—not even bringing down their own waste in the morning.

On the first floor of the Homer house, there was a large kitchen where we mostly ate, and a small bathroom with a toilet and washbasin off the dining room. Toward the front of the house were the parlor, the dining room, and front porch. The parlor eventually became a bedroom, and we used the dining room for the family room. Later on, Dad got a big metal tub from a customer. It was all black on the outside from fire, but he installed it in the bathroom and we used it for bathing. Prior to that, we all took baths from a copper wash tub that Mama heated on the back of the stove. In those days, people would only take a bath once a week, and sponge the rest of the time. As kids, we often shared the same bath to save heating the water over and over. We also did not change underclothes every day as we do now. However, Mama kept us in clean clothes and insisted we wash up every day. At least we started out the day clean.

With our growing family, we actively used the front porch for living space. On Sundays, for example, my Uncle Ellis and Aunt Anne would come to visit us from San Jose, and later my cousin Sara Levin would bring her beau Isador Marcus (Gerry and Audre's parents). I can still see them sitting on the porch with my parents, gossiping in Russian. Papa and Mama would speak in Russian in the home when they had secrets from us kids. Because my two older sisters were razzed about their English when they first went to school, my parents insisted, as did my two older sisters, that we younger children only learn to speak English. So when Russian was spoken at home on Sundays, we kids and our cousins could go to the movies to see

The Perils of Pauline, and sometimes we were even given an extra nickel for an ice cream. Over the years, we only learned a few Russian, and even Yiddish, words, but we sure knew all the names of the Little Rascals. By the way, those Sunday afternoons on the porch started the family tradition of family get-togethers or picnics which I will speak of in a later chapter, and which continue still today.

Although most of my parents' discussions were spoken in Russian, we kids knew what was going on. For example, Papa never objected to Mama spending money for food, but he did object to her spending money for clothes and shoes. As part of his business, Papa used to call on the wealthy Atherton millionaire estates to buy rags, bottles or old clothes and sacks. When he came home with a load of rags, Mama would rummage through them. She would pick out the clothes that could be used for the kinder (children), as she called us. A new dress was unheard of, but our clothes, while not new, were made of the finest materials. We also used some of the old clothes for dress-up. Also, Mama would occasionally pocket some of the sales she made in the yard, and then would tell Papa she spent much less for the shoes. I think he must have known he was being fooled, but that was the way it went.

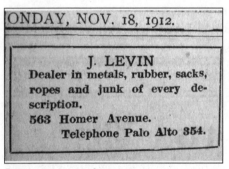

Business was expanding
(Palo Alto Historical Association)

Mama not only mended clothes, but she patched burlap sacks. Dad could get a cent more a sack with no holes. In those days, burlap sacks were used for all farm supplies and many other things, such as sugar and flour. So, besides doing the wash, cooking and mending for the family, Mama would patch the burlap bags each night—and she was either pregnant or nursing. Somehow, during this time, Mama saved enough money to buy an upright piano, which was put in the front room. She was sure one of her children would be a famous musician, given that her father was a famous violinist, and, therefore, insisted we all learn to play—mostly to no avail. My oldest sister, Esther, could pick out a tune by ear, and from then on Mama saw to it that Esther had piano lessons. She started the family tradition of music lessons from Mr.

Flint, a Stanford graduate and reputed to be a fine musician. There is more about our family music lessons in a later chapter.

At the time, I was the baby of the family. I don't know whether my older brothers just tolerated me, or if Mama made them take me with them, but I tended to ignore my two older sisters. Instead I idolized my two older brothers, and tagged along with them every chance I got. I was a total tomboy, and wore coveralls all the time before I started school, and whenever I could afterwards. At the time, I also insisted on being called Henry because I idolized my cousin Henry Levin. The best part was that my brothers included me in their games—and what games they were. We played cops and robbers in the secondhand cars my dad had in the junkyard. Generally, we kids made our own toys: scooters out of wooden boxes with wheels on the bottom—just like our heroes, the Little Rascals. Those were happy days on Homer Avenue!

The Stanford campus was also a place of fantasy and fun for my brothers and me. We loved to walk to "the farm", and play cowboys and Indians. I can recall that, every year, after the first good rain in the

The Junkman's kids: Clockwise: Esther, Elaine, Irving, Louise, David (I'm the one with the dirty face)

49

autumn, my brothers and I would head to the Stanford fields, just about where the football stadium is located now, next to El Camino Real. At that time, they kept cows at the site, so we would head out with great big buckets and pick mushrooms which were plentiful because of all the cow manure. We used to get buckets of them. Mama used to call them "shremlach" (what that means, I don't know). She believed if you cooked the mushrooms with a silver dollar, and if the silver dollar didn't turn black, then the mushrooms were safe to eat. Notwithstanding that mushrooms are difficult to identify positively, and that plants found in the wild should be positively identified before they are eaten, apparently the mushrooms we found on our yearly excursions were all non-poisonous, because we lived to tell the tale.

Friday evenings (Shabbat) we ate in the dining room, which also was used when we had company. Papa would always be served first, and then Mama served everybody else. Mama would eat last, but she was never really able to sit down and enjoy a meal because she usually had a baby in one arm. As I have mentioned previously, men were not expected to do any kind of housework, so all the cleaning up was done by the second-class citizens: the girls. I can remember Esther, as a relatively young girl, standing on a box to wash dishes, and Elaine sweeping the floor after dinner. And remember, hot water did not come out of the tap: Mama had to heat water for dishes (and the laundry) on the wood cook stove. Speaking of laundry, Mama washed clothes and boiled diapers every day!

It wasn't just family and friends that ate at our home. Hobos knew to come to our door, sometimes looking for work, but most of the time because they knew Mama would feed them. It was only years later that I understood that the hobos left marks on our house, or nearby, to let others know that our home was an easy touch, and that they would be fed. Speaking of people with their hands out, at that time religious Jews rode the trains, and stopped off at the various towns to locate Jewish families from whom to solicit donations. In Palo Alto, they were directed to Jake Levin's house—we were the town's Jews. As a result, we had a steady stream of Orthodox Jews stopping at our door and asking for funds for Israel (or Palestine, as it was known then). Papa always said he doubted much of the money ever went beyond the solicitor's pockets.

In addition to the transients who made their way to our door, our family acquired some regulars. One was called Peggy, who had a wooden peg leg and was an alcoholic. He was an extremely good worker when he wasn't drunk, but, by times, he would be locked up because of his drunk and disorderly behavior. Eventually my parents let him put up a cot and sleep in the stable. On one occasion when Papa was away, a customer came to the yard and wanted somebody to haul their junk away immediately. Mama, notwithstanding her poor English, and pregnant, still knew how to make a good deal and was determined to make the sale. She had Peggy get the horse and wagon, and the two of them drove off—with dust flying—to get the merchandise.

I guess my favorite dish from those days was Mama's stuffed cabbage rolls, sweet and sour. There are lots of versions of Mama's recipe for rolled cabbage, but the one I like best is the one she gave to Winnie when she and David were first married.

*****

Cabbage Rolls

For the broth
1 or 2 cans of chopped tomatoes)
10-20 ginger snaps (to taste)
1 quart water
1 onion, sliced
2 cloves garlic
1/2 cup lemon juice
1/2 cup brown sugar
30 cents of brisket (about 1 lb.)

For the rolls
1 1/2 pound of ground chuck
1 large onion, grated
1 large potato, grated
salt and pepper (to taste)
big cabbage

For the broth, take the canned tomatoes, add the water. Slice the onion into the water, adding the garlic, lemon juice, and brown sugar. Start to boil.

Then add brisket and cook for 1 to 2 hours at low heat. The meat will blend in with the sauce.

Mix ground meat with the grated potato and grated onion, salt and pepper. Wash, then steam the cabbage slightly, so leaves can be peeled from the head. Put two heaping tablespoons of the meat mixture (more or less depending on the size of the cabbage leaf) in the middle of the cabbage leaf, roll up, and using a toothpick to bind the leaf, if necessary. Put the filled cabbage leaves into the broth and cook for 1 to 1 ½ hours, slowly. Add the ginger snaps (to taste) for thickening, just before done, and cook for 15 minuits more.

******

The Family Keeps Growing

I remained the baby of the family for three and a half years, and because a new baby was always the center of attention, I presume I was jealous of my new baby sister, Dora, when she was born. Dorie, as she was called, was a very beautiful baby and everyone raved about her golden curls and pretty brown eyes. I suppose, because I was not noticed as much, I began to feel like an ugly duckling, and I became even more of a tomboy, refusing to play with any girls or to look after my baby sister. When Dorie was about six months old, she became very ill and had an unusually high fever. I remember a night we were all made to be very quiet and not quarrel. At the request of our family doctor, Dr. Ray Lyman Wilbur, who later would become President of Stanford University, made a home visit at night (which was very unusual), and he diagnosed Dorie as having erysipelas. Fortunately, he was able to save her, but Dorie was ill for a long time afterward, and we all sure had a scare. After that, I, too, looked after my baby sister.

As for the ebb and flow of my family's health, it was in the house on Homer that all we kids had the measles. Mama drew the shades and kept us upstairs in the one large bedroom, because she was afraid that the light would harm our eyes with the measles. Another time, we came down with whooping cough: Mama put a spoon down our throats, and brought us to the window to try to stop us from choking—doctoring us, of course, with lots of chicken soup. Speaking of doctors, anytime Mama had to call a doctor to attend to one of us, before he could leave, the rest of us were lined up by the door for a quick check-up. Mama always knew how to get her money's worth.

A few years later, when we lived on Emerson Street, my brother Irving developed scarlet fever and was put in quarantine by the doctor, with a "Quarantine" sign posted in front of our house. However, we kids would bring him the National Geographic magazines and all the funny papers that we salvaged from the junk yard. In those days, National Geographic often featured bare-breasted beauties from "primitive" lands, and my brothers really enjoyed those pictures. They called them, "BBB's". David and I would read the magazines after Irving was finished. Some quarantine! No wonder we also had slight cases of scarlet fever.

I ran away from our Homer Avenue home when I was five or six. I had been playing with my older brothers under the house, and I had found a bottle of peroxide, which I managed to break. I was afraid I would be scolded by Mama, and spanked by Papa, who had a quick temper and never had problems using the strap, so I ran away. Ely, the black chimney sweeper, was a friend of the family, so I went to his home because I knew I would be safe there. When it became dark and my family realized I was not home, they started looking for me. My sister Elaine eventually found me at Ely's house and took me home, holding my ear and scolding me all the way. When I got home, Dad wanted to whip me but Mama protected me. But I was sure scared—I never ran away again.

Although I don't remember the incident from my childhood, my mother told me that when we lived on Homer, and Dorie was quite young, she got pregnant again. Mama took Dorie (who must have been a toddler at the time) with her to the steam baths at the St. Francis Hotel in San Francisco. I think Mama believed that if she sat in the steam bath for the day, she might abort. Apparently some lady saw Dorie, and asked who this adorable child belonged to. The attendant pointed to Mama, and said that she was pregnant again and was hoping to miscarry. The lady got furious, kicked over the hot-water bucket Mama had her feet in, and supposedly said, "How could you want to miscarry when you have a child as beautiful as that?" I guess Mama took her words to heart, because she packed up my sister and they took the train back home.

Richard, the Preemie, is Born

1915 was a special year. The Panama Canal had just been opened, World War I was ravaging Europe, the World's Fair came to San Francisco, and my brother Richard was born.

During the summer of that year, our family took a day off and went to the World's Fair. Because we never had much leisure time, this was a memorable experience, especially for a young child like myself. Mama was pregnant, but was enthusiastic about the adventure. She packed a lunch, helped get us dressed in our best, and we all got on the train to San Francisco. From there we took a streetcar to the site, which was located in the Marina District, and spent the day walking around and looking at the exhibitions. One, which I particularly remember, was the Tower of Jewels. I was so impressed that I bought a pencil box with a picture of the Tower on it, which I valued for many years. My parents were keenly interested in the exhibition on the Panama Canal, and also took time to look at the new scientific instruments on display.

Shortly thereafter, Richard was born on September 1, 1915. I can recall the events leading up to his birth like it was yesterday. By then, Papa had a pickup truck that he used for the business. He made a trailer to hook onto the back, with benches in it, so that he could take us for a ride on Sundays. Anytime he took a turn, the whole thing would whip

Alpine Inn: Oldest Operating Tavern in California (Papa did business with the owners)
(Palo Alto Historical Association)

around, and while at the time it seemed like it was a lot of fun, by today's standards, it was very unsafe. On the day before Richard was born, Papa was heading to see the man who owned the Alpine Inn (a bar that later was called Rossotti's and, I recently learned, the oldest tavern in continuous operation in California). The tavern was always a favorite hangout for Stanford students. More to the point, Dad often met the owner on business – probably about old bottles – and to drink and shmooze.

Mama was very pregnant. Esther was 14, and Elaine was around 12, and they were being very sophisticated. They would actually get down on the floor and hide, because they were so embarrassed to be seen riding in Dad's homemade trailer as we went through the Stanford campus on the way to Alpine Road. My brothers and I teased them constantly! Unfortunately, Papa hit the hill leading up to Alpine Road, and the truck slid to the side of the road. Papa, who was a terrible driver, couldn't budge the truck, so he uncoupled the trailer, and he and Mama pushed the truck out of the ditch. They continued on their way, and we kids played amongst the oak trees and generally waited by the side of the road until they returned.

That night, Mama went into labor early. My brothers Irving and David and I were sent to Mrs. Tyler's home early the next day. It was a hot September day, and we and her two grandchildren sat in a circle and played under a big oak tree. The snapshot of us highlights Mrs. Tyler's mother, who looks so sedate in her rocking chair.

Esther and Elaine, who always shared the responsibilities of raising their young siblings, remained at home during Mama's labor and took care of baby Dorie. Later in the afternoon, we came home, and were told we had a baby brother. Richard, being premature, only weighed three pounds. His finger and toenails were not completely developed. He initially had to be fed with an eyedropper for about a week. Interestingly, incubators for preemies had just been intro-

The day Richard was born: David, Louise, two friends, Irving being read to at the Tylers

duced and my parents had seen one at the World's Fair. The doctor advised my parents to place him in an incubator, but my mother was convinced she could do a better job of caring for her newborn than a fancy machine.

Richard's baby bassinet was lined with cotton. To keep him warm, the practical nurse who came to the house to help Mama would open the oven door and place the basket on it. My brother David said that the first time he saw the nurse do this, he was certain she was going to bake the baby, and caused a fuss until Mama told him it was all right.

Actually, Mama was a born psychologist. To start with, Mama, when pregnant, had each of us feel the baby move in her belly. She believed we needed to know where babies came from, and it wasn't the stork! Once the new baby was born, giving the baby a bath was a ritual we all shared. Mama would take out the tin tub and place it on the kitchen table. One of the older girls would pour in the warm water. Another child would hand her the soap and a washcloth. Sometimes she would let a child wash the hands or feet of the baby. After the baby was washed, another child would hand her the warm towel, and another, the olive oil to rub the baby. The last ritual was the powder, which another child would sprinkle on the baby. In these ways, Mama let us share in the joy of the new baby, and she instilled in us all a feeling of love for the new child, instead of resentment or jealousy.

Shortly after Richard was born, we had a photo of the whole family taken in early 1916. I was seven at the time, and it was taken in our Homer Avenue house. I remember the occasion very well. We were all dressed up to go to a wedding in San Jose. My uncle Sam Edelstein (see the chapter on Mama's family) was marrying my father's niece, Dora Levin, and we were all turned out in our best and especially clean. Mama arranged to have the photo taken of the whole family by a professional photographer. Papa was upset because he thought Mama was being extravagant, but she was insistent and lots of Russian was spoken that day. As a result, all of us were very serious when the photo was taken; not a single smile on any face. Notice the button shoes on my brothers, and the short pants. Also, notice the white dresses and white shirts of the boys—all this was before Clorox!

As I mentioned earlier, relations were often strained between Mama ("the greenhorn") and Anne, the mother of the bride. My aunt did not want the five younger children (including Richard, the baby) to attend the wedding, but Mama had become strong-willed by then, and insisted: "If my children are not invited, we will

The Jacob Levin Family: Taken the day Dora Levin married Sam Edelstein, 1916
Back row: Esther, Elaine, Papa (seated), David. Front row: Irving, Mama, Richard, Louise, Jacob,
Dorie Missing: Jeanette and Sydney who were born later.

not come!" In the end, my sisters, Esther who was 15, and Elaine, 13, ate with the adults. The rest of us children played outside in the garden, which was just fine with us. I do remember that, as the bride walked down the steps, all of us kids loudly giggled and whispered, "Here comes the bride, big, fat and wide. Here comes the groom, skinny as a broom." I also can remember my parents telling us to hush up.

One of the last big events I remember on Homer came shortly before we moved away from there. My parents hired some painters to oil the shingles. I seem to remember that the oil was too thick, so the painters asked Mama if they could heat the oil on the wood cook stove. Somehow, the oil caught on fire and Mama—never one to panic—grabbed the flaming bucket with her bare hands and threw it outdoors.

In the meantime, someone must have notified the volunteer fire department. While the incident was not funny, what happened next could have been a movie. It was raining, and because most of the streets in Palo Alto were not paved, it was muddy. The bucket of oil was burning—sending sparks everywhere—and the workmen left the scene to get help. Worse yet, no fire truck arrived, although we heard the siren nearby. It turned out that the fire truck was stuck in the mud about a block from our house! By the time the fire truck finally arrived at the house, Mama—with Richard in her arms—had already put out the fire. Mama's badly burned hands soon healed, but when Jeanette was born a couple of years later with a red mark on her forehead (which rapidly faded) Mama insisted that it was a result of that fire!

Mama holding baby Richard

Happily, shortly after Richard was born, Mama and Papa were able to pay off the mortgage on Homer Avenue. Apparently, Papa had made some pretty good business deals, and he brought home some gold pieces. I don't know how he got them, nor do I remember the day, but David said he remembers Mama throwing the gold pieces up in the air with joy. It meant security and progress. David also told me that after they went to the bank and paid off the loan, Mama ripped up the mortgage document, danced a little jig, and said that Richard had brought the family "good luck". In looking back, I think my folks believed that they had saved enough for the future, and that they would never be dependent on their children.

School Days

For Mama and Papa, education was important. Indeed, from the inception of the town, many early Palo Alto residents were committed to quality elementary and secondary education. Obviously, this community interest in education had a great deal to do with Stanford University being just down the road. For many, the local schools were seen as an important stepping-stone to university entrance. As for my parents, their goal was for us to get a good education, finish high school, and in doing so, learn how to make a living. For them "making a living" was the end point. Not surprisingly, my youngest brother Sydney was the only one of us kids who completed a university degree.

Now that I look back at my parents' lack of emphasis on higher education, their orientation had a great deal to do with why my brothers, sisters and I thought it was so important for our children and grandchildren to complete their university degrees. That is not to say making a living is not important; in fact, our family has prospered because of this work ethic. But we kids wanted our children to have opportunities we knew we missed as young adults.

Mama, who never learned how to read or write English (she read Russian, Hebrew and Yiddish), certainly encouraged us to do well in school, she also thought it was a great honor to be able to skip a class. In her eyes, it proved to others you were smart, and it meant you could get an education that much faster. Of course, she praised all of us mightily when we brought home good report cards. Papa, who was always working, and often away during some of each week, had little time to celebrate our academic achievements.

From the outset of our schooling it was important for my parents, especially Mama, to be near the school. In fact, one of the reasons Mama was so pleased about the house on Homer, even though it was quite small for our growing family, was that the grammar school was across the street, and she could keep an eye on us. And

Playing at Homer Avenue School: Dorie, Louise, David, Irving, Cousin Bobby, Elaine and neighbor (from bottom to top)

from the point of view of us kids, one of the great things about our house on Homer was that, living across the street from the Homer Avenue School (now the site of Channing House), we had full-time access to the playground. We got to play on the swings and seesaws in the schoolyard whenever we had free time. We also played in the empty lot next door, where there was a cow pastured for some of the time we lived on Homer. Let me tell you, when that cow gave birth, we kids checked it out very closely. Between Mama and the babies, the dogs in the neighborhood that roamed freely, the livestock which lived nearby—and Papa's dirty jokes—we had our sex education very early! So much for the birds and the bees.

Initially the square block between Cowper Street, Homer, and Channing contained almost all of the original Palo Alto school system—the high school was at that site, as well as the intermediate school, and, of course, the Homer Avenue Grammar School. It wasn't until 1918 that the new Palo Alto High School was built at its present site on the corner of Embarcadero and El Camino Real. There was another public elementary school on Lytton Avenue, and there were several private schools such as Miss Harker's Day School and Castilleja, an all-girls school (grades 6-12), which is still in operation today. There was also the Palo Alto Military Academy where some boys boarded, but most were day students from the town.

The original Homer Avenue Grammar School only had four grades, but there was both a low and high grade in each class. Kindergarten was an innovation that started much later. When my sisters, brothers and I attended school there, one teacher was responsible for both the low and high grades, although the class sizes varied. The teachers arranged our lessons so that one part of the class would do book work and drills, while the other part of the class was more actively taught.

School had a definite routine. Each day, one teacher would ring a hand bell two times to call us in from the playground. On the second ring, all the children would line up in our grades; the girls in one line and the boys in another. At the teacher's signal, we then would march into our respective classrooms. Once in the classroom, the first thing we students did each day was to say our Pledge of Allegiance. After the pledge, we would sing, "We are all in our places with sun-shining faces," and then we would sit down to work quietly until recess. The teachers were very strict, and there was little in the way of behavior or discipline problems at school, or a ruler was used. We were all there to learn—that was the key to success. Those were the days of the "three R's", and our recreation was reading.

Esther and Elaine start school

Esther was the first one of us to start at Homer Avenue School. Her English was almost non-existent when she started, because my parents initially only spoke Russian at home. Esther said that her teachers would speak to her in English, and she would answer in Russian, and then once she learned some English, she combined the two languages. The first years at school must have been difficult for Esther, and it didn't help that she had a hearing loss because of a mastoid infection in her ear. The following year, Elaine joined her at school, and I remember my

61

sisters saying that they both were teased about their poor English. Whether Esther and Elaine instigated the change, I don't know, but from then on we spoke English at home. Elaine was very bright, quickly learning English, and soon outperformed Esther in school. Indeed, Esther only finished grammar school.

Elaine for some reason never finished her courses at high school, and, at age 16, she went to work at Cashel's Plumbing, which was located at Homer and Channing. Although Elaine seemed to have no problems with the Cashels, Papa couldn't say, "Mrs. Cashel" without also saying that, "The angels didn't want her, and the Devil was afraid of her." In a small town, we all knew everybody's business, and we all sure knew she ran her family, and the business, with an iron fist. The Cashels' home is still standing, lovingly cared for, across the street from the popular market, Whole Earth Foods, on the corner of Homer and Emerson. It is one of the few old homes left in old downtown Palo Alto.

Irving, who was a born bookworm, started at Homer Avenue School a couple of years later. He was the scholar of the family and always excelled in school. Two years later, David started at Homer Avenue School, and the following year, I started. Three years later, Dorie was the last one of the Levins to attend elementary school there. It is amusing now, but as a very young child, prior to starting school, I was often scared and would run and hide behind Mama's skirts because I could hear all the

David and Irving about 9 and 11 (taken at Alum Rock Park)

high-school kids yelling at a rally. Once I was old enough to go to school, that soon changed.

I particularly remember my second grade teacher, Miss White. I thought she was beautiful, and idolized her, and I guess Miss White must have thought I was a good student because she had me skip high second. I am not sure if I was all that brainy, but I was a very conscientious student, and I was always determined that I would do well and make my parents proud of me. Mathematics was especially easy for me. I never could understand why it was so hard for my children and even at times difficult for my grandchildren!

Some years later, when we lived on Emerson Street, and I was at Lytton School, I was sent to Dr. Black, the eye doctor who lived on University Avenue. After a long examination (there was no lens machine in those days), it was discovered that I had very poor vision, and I got my first pair of glasses. While I was always a hard worker at school, I must have then done better with the glasses, because I was skipped a grade, and was even excused from taking exams that year. I can remember the rest of the kids taking examinations, and I am certain that I was not well liked as I sat there reading a book. My brothers teased me endlessly about getting out of exams, and I loved this attention because they were the only close friends I had at the time. As I mentioned elsewhere in this book, I wasn't a very attractive child, because I was fat, wore horn- rimmed glasses, and was not interested in being feminine or graceful. My beautiful younger sister, Dorie, who was very popular and who seemed to always receive accolades for her beauty, made me more determined as a pre-teen to become an even better student and excel at something that nobody else had achieved in the family.

If Irving was the scholar, and I was the math whiz, David was the real hard worker, and he did his work quickly. I think he may have had a serious ear infection while in elementary school, because from Lytton School, David (who had been a year ahead of me) and I moved on together to the intermediate school back at Homer and Channing. I had jumped a year, but upon entering intermediate school I received my first lesson in academic humility. In our first year, all girls had to take home economics, and the boys took machine shop. David excelled in shop (it was like being in the junkyard), but I barely passed because I was so uncoordinated and unusually poor at sewing. In fact, I ran a needle though my finger at one point, and was sent by a disgusted teacher to the nurse for repairs. I probably just passed home economics because I could cook—Mama saw that all her girls were good cooks.

In a similar vein, during our first year in intermediate school, my brother David and I were put in the same French class. Our teacher was Miss. Fenwick, who spoke beautiful French, but it didn't matter because it turned out that I was not good at languages. At one point, I rebelled and didn't do my homework, but David did, so I copied David's French lesson to be able to turn in my paper. Good ol' David. The teacher gave him hell for copying my paper, but he never squealed on me. It was a difficult year for me in French. It was one of my weak spots—one of them. The other was in music. I have since learned that it has been found that people who are tone-deaf have great difficulty learning to speak foreign languages.

Music Lessons

Of all my siblings, Esther was the most musical. She loved to play the piano, which she did as much as she could throughout her life. Anybody could hum a tune, and Esther could pick out the notes and soon play the tune. Elaine took the violin for a time, but gave it up for boys by the time she was a pre-teen. My two older brothers were exempted from music lessons because they helped Papa in the junkyard. I was next! I can remember my first attempt at singing in class. My very attractive teacher, named Miss Lee, would walk down the aisle and make encouraging suggestions to each student. When she would come to me, she'd just look at me and say, "Please don't sing." I still can't carry a tune, although I have always loved music. I just can't produce it. It was too bad because Mama had hopes that one of us would become a great musician. Yet, that didn't deter her from ensuring that I took piano lessons from Mr. Flint for a few years and, unlike many other children, I really did practice. The poor man. I think he practically pulled his hair out. I just didn't have it. I still remember the last piece that I had to learn; it was from "The Tales of Hoffman". I was just a sad, sad, case, and must have murdered the piece. After that, Mr. Flint told my mother it was a waste of money to try and teach me. Obviously, I was not one of the musicians that Mama hoped for.

Dorie took music lessons from Mr. Flint too. She definitely had more musical talent than I did, and seemed to enjoy playing the piano. Her great musical moment came the year she played a duet at a recital with her friend, Eva Enten. All the rest of us kids attended the recital, very proud of our younger sister. Esther (who was like a second mom to Dorie) had specially done up her hair, and Dorie was wearing a freshly pressed dress. We kids all marched into the Women's Club (it is still there on the corner of Homer and Cowper) expecting something special. It was, but not what we expected. Eva, our sister's partner, was very heavy as a child—fat, actually—and she ended up taking almost all of the piano bench. In the end, we heard the duet, but all anybody could see were four hands and Eva. It has been a family joke ever since.

Palo Alto High School

What Palo Alto High School looked like in 1926
(Madrono, Palo Alto High School Yearbook, 1926)

After intermediate school, both David and I (still in the same class) moved on to Palo Alto High School. David never was interested in high school, and never really performed academically. He also rarely had anything to do with after-school activities because, as soon as he got through with his classes, he was expected to come home and work in the junkyard. Actually, David was shy, but that being said, he loved to tease the girls, and was a very handsome young man with beautiful curly hair, and all the girls really liked him. As she aged, Helen Larsen, my girlfriend and older sister of Virginia (Sydney's future wife), often told a story about what it was like to sit in front of David in high school. Helen was a serious student, and had these beautiful, blonde, long braids of which she was very proud—almost vain. David constantly teased her about being so serious, and never missed the opportunity to tease her about her braids. By times, when he was bored, he would dip the tips of her hair into his ink well—á la Tom Sawyer—just to get her mad at him.

Irving's High School Graduation 1923

Around this time, Irving, who was the first of the Levins to graduate from high school, told my parents that he wanted to become a lawyer. He had saved enough money working at the junkyard to enroll at Stanford University, which welcomed Palo Alto graduates to attend. While there was still no tuition charged in those days because of the generous endowment of Mr. Stanford, Irving had saved approximately $100 for expenses. He was very excited about his education. Then, as is described in another chapter, he said he was hit with a lightning bolt—falling in love with Yetta Haber. They soon married, and he went back to work at the junkyard.

With this as background, by the time I entered high school I loved to learn, and looked forward to high school, although it started out, and ended, rather badly. On my first day, as a new student in grade 10—I can still so vividly remember the affront—one of the teachers, Miss Montgomery, confronted me and said, right off the bat, "Isadore (Irving) was one of my brightest students. I don't expect you to do as well. Girls never do." Notwithstanding her comments, I excelled in mathematics, of course, and did well in English and social studies, too.

Toward the end of high school, I can remember one of my teachers (I guess she was a counselor) asking me what I was going to do now that I was finishing my studies. I said I was going to find a job and work before going to university. She was quite anxious to know why I didn't go on to Stanford immediately, because, although tuition was now charged, it was still nominal, and she stressed that I had scored so well on my pre-college entrance tests. Unfortunately, I was a product of my time and, as I have said elsewhere, it was more important in my family for a boy to get an education than a girl. Thus, although I have had a lifelong interest in learning, and have continually taken night-school courses, I never did get to university. (Note: In her mid-80s, Louise was studying comparative religions, current events and computers.)

In 1926, I became the first of the Levin girls to graduate high school, although it was touch and go just before I was to graduate. Always on the lookout for a good joke, towards the end of my senior year, I gave Feenamint gum (a laxative) to one of the girls in my class. I can't remember why I did that, but she reported me to the principal once she could get off the pot. The funniest thing about that incident is that I had forgotten about it until saw this woman at a 1995 Palo Alto High School reunion. She came striding up to me and asked if I still played dirty tricks on people.

I don't remember much about Dorie and Jeanette in school, although I know that Dorie was very popular in high school and had lots of friends. After graduating from high school, Dorie started junior college in San Mateo, but, because it was during the worst of the Depression, she soon had to stop school and start work to help out the family. As for Jeanette, she was ten years younger than me, and unfortunately I don't remember much about her schooling or lessons.

Louise's High School Graduation, 1926

Richard playing in the School Band (second row in the middle) (Palo Alto Historical Association)

By the time Richard attended Palo Alto High School, he was very popular and a good student. He, too, helped out at the junkyard, as well as promoting his own business, which was buying and selling burlap sacks around the area. Richard was always creative, and always had at least 10 things on the go. He didn't go out for sports when he was in high school, but he always had a development project going in our garden (a rockery, a pond and a miniature golf course, for example), and he had time to form and, of course, promote Dick Levin's Orchestra. Richard played the saxophone, and his group used to play at the noon dances and occasionally elsewhere. While always active, Richard also was always chubby. His close friends nicknamed him "Hippo", which sure didn't slow him down with the girls. He must have had quite a line, because there were usually lots of them around.

After graduating from high school (again, because it was during the Depression), Richard moved to San Jose where he joined David, who by this time was working with Henry (Ellis's son) in the junk business. He soon was making deals and finding new markets for the junk (now called salvage) business which, in its time, grew to be the largest of its kind on the West Coast.

It was during the time when Richard was in high school that my future husband Fred starting courting me. One of the first times he came to call, Richard and the rest of his "orchestra" were practicing in our living room on Channing Avenue. Imagine the noise. And, not to be outdone, Sydney—Mama's current musical hope—was playing a completely different piece of music on the violin, going up and down the stairs, and telling Mama at the same time he had practiced long enough. Fred could hardly believe the cacophony, but when he came back, I figured he was a keeper.

Sydney, the youngest of the nine kids, was the only one of us who went beyond high school. Syd did well in school because he was always interested in learning new things. As a young teen, he would try anything. He plucked chickens to earn spending money; worked for a nursery; had gardening jobs in the neighborhood, and helped Richard with his burlap-sack route. I remember that while Syd was still in high school, Ted Smolen, who had recently married Dorie,

The brothers: Richard, Sydney and David, 1943

got him interested in photography, and also taught him to box. As a result, Syd became the high-school photographer, built a darkroom off the garage on Channing Avenue, and learned to beat up the schoolyard roughnecks who were harassing him.

Syd graduated from Palo Alto High School in 1940, and that summer, he and his good friend Fred Cruise drove all the way to the Yucatan in Mexico. It was quite an adventure. They were robbed, saw the sights, and, as Syd still says, he and Fred learned to listen to waiters in foreign lands after insisting on ordering the most expensive item on the menu which turned out to be stuffed worms.

That next fall, Syd started his first year of college at San Jose State, and then, in his second year, he transferred to the University of California, at Davis. At the time, he wanted to focus on agriculture. By then, World War II was under way, and he joined the Navy in 1942, hoping to get into officer training. Syd said that when he was asked for his mother's maiden name he thought for a minute and said, "McFadden" (Irish for Dickenfadden). He now credits his "Irish" ancestors for his success in the Navy, because shortly after, he was sent to a Midshipman College in Chicago, and ended up as a lieutenant on a supply ship near Australia. Fortunately, he didn't see actual combat, and he says that the only scary (and educational) experience he had was in New Guinea—he had an unfortunate encounter with a huge tattooed protector of a beautiful bare breasted beauty (BBB's again!).

Eventually Syd finished his university education at Stanford. Ever the equestrian, he would occasionally ride Big Red, one of the horses from our ranch (located just behind the Stanford campus), to classes. He tells a funny story about hanging out at the ranch and then realizing he was late for class. He galloped down the hill to the Campus, and ended up having to tie Big Red to the bushes in front of Hoover Tower so he could make it to class in time. The best part of the story is that, when he came out after class, there was no Big Red, no bushes, but there was a big pile of horse pucky left on the steps of Hoover Tower. He sure hightailed it out of there real fast! As Mama would say, just another vote for the "Respublicans".

In looking back at our education, all of us were taught the love of reading, to value work, to appreciate sound knowledge, and to ask questions. Papa constantly brought home books for us to read that he acquired in his junk business, and we were encouraged to use the library. Mama, through example, taught us that to be idle is a disgrace. Both Papa and Mama taught us to make considered choices, and to focus on the important. They taught us to value family (to always be there for each other in good times and bad). They also taught us to respect all races and religions, and the importance of service, whether in support of religion, of children, of education, or of the poor.

Finally, no discussion of education can be complete without the subject of politics. Politics was part of the diet of our everyday life. Because of my parents' immigrant background, they were internationalists by birth, and taught us to be so by example. As I have mentioned elsewhere, Mama subscribed to the *Jewish Forward* and shared the news with us. Papa and my older brothers read the local papers and shared the news with us. My parents, of course, followed events in Europe carefully and encouraged us to do so as well. I can remember huddling around one of our first radios (it was a used radio) and listening for the news. Moreover, our parents taught us that to be able to vote was a privilege; it was the hallmark of a democracy, and it was the true sign of a citizen. So, one had to discuss the voting choices, and the options—usually at the dinner table.

Many years later, after Mama had moved to the corner of Cowper and Oregon Avenue, my brothers gave her a television (first a black-and-white, and then one in color). Mama was overjoyed at being able to watch the news on television, especially her favorite, Edward R. Murrow. From then on, at least twice a day, she never failed to watch the news, and educational and current events programs. Her recreational viewing was restricted to watching Ed "Solomon" (Sullivan) on Sunday nights and, as she got older, Liberace. To the end, Mama would discuss current events with young and old alike, and she never failed to have an opinion.

I thank my parents for the gift of education, and for the belief that we kids had the ability and responsibility to not only to make a living, but to make a difference.

Growing Up Jewish In Early Palo Alto

As I write what it was like to be Jewish in Palo Alto at the beginning of the last century, I am mindful that at the beginning of the twenty-first century, Palo Alto is a multi-ethnic and multi-cultural community with a Jewish population of approximately 20 percent. When we Levin kids were growing up, Palo Alto was a very traditional, white, Christian community, and because of that, we knew we were different. While there may have been a Jewish traveling merchant who lived for a time in Mayfield, it was well known in Palo Alto and the surrounding region that Jake Levin and his family were the town's Jews. As a result, Mama was always careful to instruct us to behave, because she wanted everyone in town to respect us and our religious beliefs. She made sure that we were always scrubbed and immaculately clean when we went to school, and Mama and Papa took great pains to ensure their word was good, and that they were respected by our clients and our neighbors. In turn, we were taught to be honest and hard-working, but not to attract attention.

I am happy to be able to say that there was not a lot of overt anti-Semitism in Palo Alto when we were growing up, although there was overt discrimination against the Chinese, who were not allowed to own land, and there was racism toward the Japanese and Filipinos as well. The few African-American families there were in Palo Alto in the early 1900s must have also experienced the discrimination of the times, although I don't really know, because my parents were friendly with all races, and they all had a seat at our dining table.

As children on our own, occasionally we did encounter rude comments. Several incidents involved the Hardeman family who lived next door to us at 541 Homer Avenue. They were very observant Catholics, and their kids were toughies who gave us continual grief as young children. One time, they came home from church and started throwing rocks at us, and called us Christ-killers. That just made us mad, and we fought with them. Another time, we were called dirty Jews by the same neighbors. Fortunately their priest, Father Gleason, was passing by, and he laced into the neighbor kids for calling us names. I don't remember what happened after that, but I do know they stopped the religious taunting. The interesting thing is that Mama later told me that Mrs. Hardeman was born a Jew, but converted to Catholicism. As it turned out, one of the Hardeman kids became a priest, and another was a teacher, and yet another became a violinist. I am certain they became more tolerant as adults, but as kids they sure were tough on their Jewish neighbors.

After the incident with the Hardeman kids and the priest, David, Irving and I became curious about Catholics—what they were like, what were their rituals, etc. Shortly after, I remember going with my older brothers to the Catholic Church at Homer and Waverley Streets to see what it was like inside. We sneaked in and looked at the holy water, and even tasted it. We saw a large picture of Jesus, and we stood in awe of this larger-than-life figure on a cross. We did not stay long, feeling that we were doing a dangerous act, but the visit satisfied our curiosity.

Another incident, and one that affected me directly, was my high-school English teacher instructing me in front of the class that I would know how to read Shylock in the Merchant of Venice. At the time, I was mortified because of the anti-Semitic content in the play. My brother Richard also had some difficulty with the football coach at high school, who made continual anti-Semitic comments because Richard (like my older brothers) did not turn out for after-school sports. Typically, Richard just ignored him, but I know it hurt him deeply. In thinking about this subject, I am certain, given my parents' background, my mother kept her ears open to make sure we kids were allowed to grow up free of religious fear, and to ensure we did not encounter much overt prejudice. I do remember as a child, that Mama always encouraged us to be proud of our heritage and religion notwithstanding what others may have said.

In looking back at our life in those days, it seems to me that although Mama was deeply religious, our lifestyle had as much to do with being Jewish as did religion in the formal sense. This may have been the result of being the town's only Jews for many years; it may have been because of Papa's lack of interest in formal religion, or it may have been the result of my parents' desire to have their children be Americans. Whatever the reasons, for Mama (who was observant) and in turn for us, being Jewish meant celebrations and rituals of food and friends and love, rather than adherence to religious protocols.

For example, we didn't keep a kosher home (Mama couldn't have even if she wanted to, because the only kosher meat to be found came from San Francisco or Oakland), but we never ate pork or shellfish products at home. Yet, Mama generally tried to keep kosher throughout her life and, notwithstanding our somewhat unique dietary practices, when the Jewish holidays came, Mama would always make sure that our teachers and our friends knew it was a special time for us. For example, when Passover came, we kids would bring matzoh to school, so that our teachers and classmates would know that it was one of our holidays, as well as why we did not eat bread for that week. Conversely, Papa, who was not religious, had no time for any type of dietary practice. He said he walked away from all that when he left Russia. Besides, he loved bacon, and often ate it when he was out on business trips. Over time, Papa even brought bacon home and asked Mama to cook it for him, although she would never serve it to us. Thus, bacon became the "forbidden fruit" for us kids and, as adults, all of us, while still observant, have followed in my father's footsteps when it comes to food.

Passover

An early Passover at 333 Channing: Stanley, Yetta, Jeanette, Elaine, Esther

My favorite holiday is Passover. It always was a time for all the family to get together to celebrate the triumph over religious persecution, and we would always have as many guests as the room could hold. For our family, the holiday had special meaning because my parents, escaping discrimination in Russia—much like Moses leading the Jews out of Egypt—came to America as part of the great Jewish migration at the turn of the twentieth century. Quiet messages about religion and family were demonstrated to us all in the course of this holiday. And my parents, who always felt blessed to live in America, ensured they shared their blessings with family and friends.

Mama, of course, was much more religious than Papa—thus, Passover was a time of much preparation on her part. Each year, Mama would work for weeks to prepare for the Seder. As for Papa, each year he would look for ways to make the service shorter. We children loved the shorter service because we got to eat sooner, but over the years, much of the history about how the holiday was celebrated by our Russian ancestors was lost.

My best memories are of preparing for the Seder. Prior to the holiday each year, off Mama would go on a pilgrimage to McAllister Street, which was the Jewish neighborhood in San Francisco, to buy kosher foods, matzoh and other Passover goodies for the holiday. It was a big deal for her because she had to take the train to San Francisco, and then the trolley car. I am sure that she considered the day a good time because she was able to speak Russian with fellow shoppers and the merchants, but coming home must have been difficult because she always had so many bags, and, of course, she often was pregnant.

On arriving home, Mama would start preparations for the holiday by having us kids really clean the cupboards and the house, under the guise of looking for homitz (leavened flour products). In those days we didn't waste food, so any leavened bread or flour was used again after Passover—we put all the leavened food in boxes, and stored it in the basement until the end of Passover. We children loved to help Mama remove the homitz from the cupboards in preparation for the holiday. She would sing or hum while we were cleaning and she was preparing all the food. Of course, we all looked forward to the traditional meal because there was lots to eat: gefilte fish made from scratch, as it was in those days; homemade chicken soup with matzoh balls; baked chicken; new potatoes, and we always had fresh asparagus. Such excitement and joy. All the girls happily helped Mama with the cooking, setting the table and making everything shine. As Mama always said, "Don't complain, this is part of the fun."

This tradition continues today. The women in our family have always done a wonderful job of making the Seder meal. It has always been a special holiday for the family, and it must be in the genes to sweat over the hot stove, making the soup and matzoh balls, chicken and rest of the meal. The following recipe is first of the family Passover favorites.

*****

Matzoh Balls (Kneydlakh)

4 large eggs, well beaten
1 cup matzoh meal
salt and pepper to taste
chopped parsley
1 level teaspoon baking powder (my addition for a lighter texture)
1 teaspoon of rendered chicken fat, if desired

Put all the above in a bowl. Let stand about 20 minutes. Roll in small balls (larger ones can end up like rocks). Gently put all the balls into a pot of boiling water. If you have some chicken fat, put that in the water for flavor. Turn down the heat and cook for about 30 minutes in a covered pot. Today, matzoh balls can be made several days in advance of Passover, as can the chicken soup, and both kept in the refrigerator and even frozen, if space is a concern.

*****

I have two enduring Passover memories from my youth. The first, and my favorite, is when Jeanette was about seven years old. Her job was to clean up the Seder table after everyone ate, but she helped a bit more with the Seder that year than was anticipated. Jeanette, ever the helpful child, decided that year she would sample the leftovers in everyone's wineglass, and became very tipsy and very silly before she fell asleep on the floor. We all laughed at her antics and teased her about her behavior for years. Another wonderful memory I have of Passover is from when we lived on Emerson Street: Mama bought a live fish that she put in the bathtub for a day before she cooked it for gefilte fish. My two older brothers and I tormented that poor fish endlessly while it was alive, but could barely eat it once it was dead! All we could see were the fish eyes, even though we usually all loved Mama's gefilte fish, which is described below.

*****

Mama's Gefilte Fish

For the fish-ball mixture
*About 5 pounds of fresh fish (e.g. 1
    pound salmon, and the rest:
    whitefish, sole, halibut or cod)*
2 onions
1 carrot
2 teaspoons sugar
salt and pepper to taste
2 ½ cups water
2 tablespoons matzoh meal
2 eggs, well beaten

For the fish stock
*Fish bones and skins from fish ball
    mixture (including extra heads,
    if you have them)*
2 onions, quartered
2 carrots, plus addional, sliced
2 stalks celery
1 sweet potato or parsnip
2 quarts water
salt and pepper to taste
parsley

To make the stock
One half-hour before starting the fish-ball mixture, put the fish-stock ingredients in the pot, bring them to a boil, and then simmer for 2 hours. Cool and then strain.

To make the fish balls
Grind the fish, onions, carrot and sugar together in a food processor. Place in large bowl. Add salt and pepper to taste, the matzoh meal and eggs, and up to

2 1/2 cups of water. Keep mixing all the time while you add the above ingredients. (Mama would grind the fish with a hand meat grinder and chop the vegetables).

Form the mixture into balls, rolling them in hands wet with water.

Add fish balls to strained fish stock and simmer for 1 ½ hours. Add parsley and additional sliced carrots in the last 15 minutes. Cool and then refrigerate the fish balls in the stock.

To serve, place the fish balls on a bed of lettuce. To garnish, add a teaspoon of beet horseradish on the side and a slice of lemon.

*****

Of course, there was more to Passover than the Seder. Because we ate no bread for a week, Mama often would serve scrambled eggs and matzoh. However, as kids, our favorite breakfast meal during Passover was pancakes. I still make them as a treat.

*****

Mama's Passover Pancakes

2 large eggs, separated, and the whites beaten stiff
3/4 cup matzoh meal
1 cup milk
salt to taste
sugar and cinnamon to taste
butter, to fry
jam, to serve

Beat the yolks well, add the milk and matzoh meal, then sugar, salt and cinnamon. Fold in beaten egg whites. Fry in butter, serve with jam.

*****

Passover at 333 Channing: probably 1944 or 1945

The above photo of Passover was taken in our family home on Channing Avenue in 1944 or 1945. Not all of us are there. Papa and Irving had already died, and Sydney was serving in the Navy during World War II, but it was still a crowd. The dining room could not accommodate all of us, so Mama had the Seder in the living room. Kenneth Zwerin, a family friend (the de-facto first rabbi of Temple Beth Jacob), conducted the service and, believe me, it was longer than Papa's. Kenneth always made the Seder fun, as well as a history lesson for all who attended. We never knew who he would call on to read the roles of the wicked son and the stupid son, so each year, it was always a guessing game which got more rowdy with each additional glass of wine. And the singing, although often off-key, made it a very happy time.

Years later, when I was married to Fred, we often had family Seders at our home on Madrono Avenue, and then on Pitman. Fred loved Passover, too (he loved parties of all kinds), so a big Seder was an annual event. One year, when we opened the door for Elijah the Prophet, a big Irish Setter came strolling through the door, and stopped where the cup for Elijah was placed. After that, we always joked that Elijah

Julia and the Grandchildren: Passover, 1944 or 1945

was reincarnated as an Irish Setter who just lived down the block. After Fred died, I usually went to my brother Richard and his wife, Emmy Lou's, who continued the family tradition of a large family Seder party at their home in San Jose. I am sure Passover is still the favorite holiday for all the members of our family. It symbolizes the coming of new life, as well as celebrating our family's opportunity for freedom.

Julia and the Grandchildren, Passover: 1961, at Richard and Emmy's

The Sabbath

Friday night is a special night for Jews all over the world: it marks the beginning of the Sabbath. It certainly was a special night in our family, and we never missed observing it. First off, we all had to dress in clean clothes. For the Sabbath meal, we had a white linen tablecloth on the table, with the beautiful brass candlesticks Mama brought from Russia. Frequently, family and friends joined us at the Shabbat table to help celebrate. As Mama would often say, "God forbid that anybody should be alone on the Sabbath." Saturday, the actual Sabbath, was not considered a special day when we were young, and I don't recall ever seeing my family take time out to observe. Papa always worked on Saturdays—it was often the busiest day at the Yard, and Mama never had a holiday, or could take time out to be religious, with all us kids to look after.

For the Sabbath, as usual, Mama would hum while she prepared Shabbat dinner. I can still see her making the noodles for Lukshenkugel (a pudding-like dish), and baking the chala, the bread. We often had chicken soup to start on Friday nights, and Mama—never to waste a thing—would fry the boiled soup chicken in butter, or chicken fat, to give it more flavor, and serve it with vegetables for the main course. The fish man always came to Palo Alto on Fridays for the Catholic families, and he also called at our door. Because the fish was very fresh and well iced, we often had fresh fish on Fridays, including Mama's gefilte fish.

Before we sat down to the meal, Mama would don a headscarf, raise her hands in prayer and bless the candles. Papa would bless the bread and wine, and after that, we would tuck into our meal. Each week, they reminded us of our blessings (being born in the United States), and although we rarely had to be urged to clean our plates, we were always told of the starving children in Armenia.

My children, when they were young, used to ask me if we ever went hungry "in the olden days", because they knew we were poor, and there were lots of mouths to feed. My response was that we always had all the food we could eat, but we sure didn't waste. Whatever anyone took on their plate was eaten, especially the noodle pudding.

*****

Friday Night Lukshenkugel

1 package wide egg noodles, cooked
1-3 eggs, well beaten
sugar, cinnamon to taste
butter to dot

Mix all the ingredients together. Put in a well-greased glass pan, add some butter on top, and bake in a 325° oven until done, about 45 minutes to 1 hour. For variety, add 1 cup sour cream and/or raisins, apples or cottage cheese.

*****

Hanukkah

As Jews, obviously we did not believe in Christmas, and we certainly did not celebrate Christmas, nor were we taught to believe in Santa Claus. As a child, this was the only time I felt sorry for myself. Christmas was not so commercial as it is now, but it still seemed to me, when I was a child, that all the kids in the neighborhood had new toys for Christmas, and we had none. Of course there was Hanukkah, the Festival of Lights, which is at the same time of year, but when we were kids, all my family did was light the candles. There were no gifts given for eight days, as is the custom today. Nor was it considered such a special celebration as it is today. Our treat was to get Hanukkah Gelt, a piece of chocolate wrapped in gold foil to look like a gold coin, and to eat potato latkes. I believe it is a tradition for Eastern European Jews to eat food cooked in oil, such as latkes, during Hanukkah to celebrate the Festival of Lights.

The year I was about nine, my father was going to night school (we were living on Emerson Street at the time). It was just before Christmas. The school had a draw for a fully decorated Christmas tree ,and my dad won it! He was so pleased, and brought it home for us kids because he knew we would love it, and we sure did. What he did not factor into his decision was Mama, who was the religious one in the family. She insisted that he put the tree in the basement, and said we must be mindful of our own traditions, and preserve them, not those of the Christians. I think there were strong words exchanged that night on the subject, because I remember them speaking loudly in Russian. The next morning, my mother gave the decorated tree to a neighbor family, two doors down on Emerson. Although I accepted that a tree was a no-no, I was sorely disappointed. I remember feeling especially sad and very left-out that Christmas. I guess that is why it is still not my favorite time of year. That is also one of the reasons why Fred and I agreed that our children would be raised with Hanukkah, and a Christmas tree, and Santa Claus.

Today, the Christmas-Hanukkah season seems to have become an ecumenical holiday, which I consider to be a positive step, but it also has become so commercial that many have lost sight of the religious aspects and traditions of the respective holidays. However, the latkes we know and love will continue in our family, as well the stories of Judith, the honey cakes and the scrappy Maccabees.

*****

Mama's Potato Latkes

2 eggs, beaten
4 potatoes
1 onion, grated
2 tablespoons matzoh meal (or flour)
salt to taste
canola oil for frying
sour cream and applesauce, to serve

Finely grate the potatoes, draining off any accumulated moisture. Add the beaten eggs, flour, onion matzoh meal and salt. Fry in a shallow pan of hot oil until browned crisply. Today, we can cook and freeze them in advance of the family celebration. They brown nicely on a cookie sheet in a 450 oven. Serve with sour cream and applesauce.

*****

The interesting part of this story is what happened at Easter. Obviously, we did not believe in Easter, or the Resurrection, but Mama must have felt differently about the Easter Bunny. Every year, she would cook eggs, let us color them, and hide them for us to hunt. So the Easter Bunny became part of our family tradition, and, as far as I know, most of the family with young children still celebrates Easter with an Easter Egg Hunt. By the way, we knew Mama was the Tooth Fairy, but we always found a coin under our pillow, and the tooth gone.

A Place to Worship

Because we were the first Jewish family in the Palo Alto/Menlo Park area. My parents wanted to ensure we had some religious training and identity. Thus, occasionally during the year—and always for the High Holidays—our family would make the trip to Bicker Kolem, a Conservative Synagogue in San Jose, that had been started around the beginning of the twentieth century. Eventually, it became Temple Emanuel, the Reform synagogue, which has been a center of Judaism in San Jose.

In the early 1900s, the only other synagogue in the region was in San Francisco, and that was simply too far for all of us to go for a day of worship, especially before my parents were able to buy a car. More importantly, taking all us kids anywhere must have been daunting! Even the trip to San Jose for the High Holy Days was a logistic nightmare, and involved an all-day trip. Therefore it was not surprising that, once a small group of religious Jews moved to Stanford Park in Menlo Park, Mama and Papa joined with them to build a place of worship in the immediate area. But let me tell you, all this took many years of talk and planning.

Mama, ever the organizer, realized that the most effective way to begin organizing for the synagogue was to do it through the women, with the assistance of the men. Over the years, Mama held many ladies' meetings and fundraising events for the synagogue at our home. Eventually, she organized the first meeting of the Temple Sisterhood and, not surprisingly, she became the first president. Years later, Mama also organized the first Hadassah group on the Peninsula, as well as the Jewish Consumption Relief Association, which is now called City of Hope and is located in Los Angeles.

By 1927, the number of other Jewish families in the area had increased, and there were now enough men to be able to conduct services, so Temple Beth Jacob was born. There were 25 members in the new synagogue and, because there was no building, the first service was held in the living room of the Entens, one of the founding member families. There were not enough chairs, so the men stood, and the women sat around the table in the dining room. Somebody must have got a deal on used books, because the first prayer books were in Hebrew and German.

Following this inaugural service, weekly services were held in the homes of the various members. During the initial period, the men in the congregation were very involved in designing and delivering the services, but vigorous disagreements often arose on the pulpit, and this idea was abandoned by the time the synagogue was built. As well, during this time, and to help raise money for the mortgage, "alyas"

Temple Beth Jacob, Creek Drive, Menlo Park, 1933

(special prayers) were auctioned to the highest bidder. This continued for several years, including the first few years after the synagogue was built, but it was eventually stopped because of the small jealousies that arose.

Religious squabbles aside, Papa and Mama, as well as the other original families, generously gave their time and labor to see this dream become a reality. Finally, a sanctuary, with a small attached kitchen, was erected in 1933 on Creek Drive in Menlo Park, off El Camino Real, just over the border from what is now the Stanford Shopping Center. The building is no longer there, which is sad, because it had a lovely stained-glass window of the Star of David, and was built in the old Palo Alto-Spanish style, similar to the older buildings at Stanford. Many years later, in 1960, the Temple was moved to a larger site in Redwood City, where it is still located.

People still ask me why the original synagogue was in Menlo Park, and not Palo Alto, especially because Mama and Papa were so instrumental in helping to start it. The reason was practicality and compromise. Because Papa was not religious, he didn't mind driving on the Sabbath. He just wanted a place nearby where we, as a family, could worship. On the other hand, there were a number of religious Jews in the immediate neighborhood who wanted to walk to services, and to be near a kosher kitchen. Also, the synagogue drew its members from communities as far away as San Mateo in the north, to Mountain View in the south, so the original members thought it was important to locate the facility in a central location, off the main thoroughfare—El Camino Real.

Once the synagogue was finally built, our family friend Kenneth Zwerin conducted the first services. He was not only the acting rabbi, but the first Religious School teacher and chauffeur. Later on our family friend, Sid Gutterman, and his brother drove the students to and from religious school. Frankly, when Kenneth arrived on the scene, it seemed like a new beginning; the services became much less orthodox, and new prayer books in Hebrew and English were purchased.

Although Kenneth conducted the services, several of the men who were well versed in Hebrew participated in the service, and also chanted prayers for High Holidays. My favorite memory of those early days at the synagogue is of Mr. Blackman, one of the founding members, who always took out his false teeth and put them on the railing, so he could blow the shofar at High Holy Days. And how he struggled to get a sound out of that ram's horn: I used to hold my breath in anticipation, and tried not to laugh, although I was not always successful.

Originally, we had no wooden pews in the synagogue, just folding chairs. During the High Holy Days, extra folding chairs were brought in to accommodate the increased numbers of worshipers. Because it was often hot during the month of September, and the room had no air-conditioning, as well as being poorly ventilated, we all baked, as well as prayed, in the room. Early on, one of the original members, Mr. Enten, fell asleep during one of the first High Holy Day services, and crashed on to the floor, or, as Papa said, woke everybody else up.

As for the finances, Mama and Papa and others continued the fundraising for the synagogue during the early thirties—the Depression—because the mortgage on the Temple had to be paid monthly, and on time! The banks in those days were not forgiving if a loan payment was late. As a result, Mama initiated whist card-parties at the Temple to raise money for the mortgage. If we realized $20 at the end of the day, it was considered a good haul, and Mama was pleased.

Then there were the big money-raising picnics, held at the Levin Ranch, where Mama's beans were the drawing card. Unfortunately, her recipe for baked beans has been lost, but they were made with beef ribs, and they were delicious. Mama was tireless. She would not only cook for the event, but she went from merchant to merchant in Palo Alto to get the local merchants to donate prizes for the various events at the picnic. But somehow it was those pots and pots of beans that sold the best. As a teen, I was brought along to help with Mama and her fundraising efforts, and to this day, I still hate asking people to give.

But it wasn't just Mama who was active. Although Papa could hardly be called religious, he was respected. As a result, he was elected in 1927 (without contest) as the first president of the synagogue. In 1934 or 1935, shortly before Papa died, Mr. Blackman served as interim president until the congregation could hold a new election. My brother Irving was immediately elected as the second president. Unfortunately, he died in 1937 at age 31, far too young. Both deaths deeply affected not only our family, but our small Jewish community. Shortly after Irving's death, the members were able to build a reception hall beside the little sanctuary, and it was dedicated to my brother. To this day, the synagogue is called Temple Beth Jacob and Irving Levin Center.

The picture above is what the inside of the original synagogue looked like. Mama is the woman in the black dress seated on the right front. Mr. and Mrs. Gutterman, also synagogue pioneers, are next to her. Standing in the center back, from left to

1st. Installation and Banquet at The Temple of the Beth Jacob & Jewish Center. Oct. 29, 1933.

Julia seated, center right, Richard 2nd row center left, Irving & Yetta standing right of center, Kenneth Zwerin standing, left of center

right, are Mr. Blackman, Kenneth Zwerin, Manny Charnow and Mrs. Charnow (Manny owned a delicatessen in Palo Alto at the time), Irving (who must have been president at the time) and Yetta. In the far left, is Jake Schwartz, who owned Polly and Jake's (it used to be on the corner of El Camino Real and Oregon Avenue). Also, my brother Richard is sitting on the center left—he is the one with the big smile.

History has a way of repeating itself. After Fred and I were married, and had our children, we, together with cousin Gerry Marcus, became interested in participating in a more reformed approach to Judaism. Gerry who had married Eleanor (Elie) Hyman was a young lawyer and, like us, thought it was time for Palo Alto to have its first synagogue. As a result, Gerry and I, with three others, met to discuss starting a Reform Temple in Palo Alto. Gerry was elected the first president of Beth Am, and I was elected as a board member.

As a first step, we rented a small house on Forrest Avenue for an office, and for the religious school. Our first High Holy Day services were conducted with a borrowed Torah, and were held at the Buddhist Temple on Middlefield Avenue. However, it became clear that their sanctuary was too small to hold our rapidly growing congregation. Shortly thereafter, we approached the Palo Alto Baptist Church, which was located next door to our office, to see if we could rent their sanctuary on Friday nights, but they said no. We really didn't know what to do next. It was then that the local Methodist minister, Reverend Stuart, approached us to see if we wanted to use their facility. He had heard a rumor that we needed a place to hold services. Of course we jumped at the opportunity, and, over the years, our two communities developed a close inter-faith relationship.

Soon we were able to hire a full-time rabbi. My son, Stephen, was one of the first young men to have a bar mitzvah at Beth Am. It was held on a Friday night at the Methodist Church, and I can still see Fred, fussing at the last minute over the flowers on the altar. As importantly, to celebrate Stephen's bar mitzvah, Fred and I gave the first Torah to Beth Am, which Fred carried in for the first time for the service. It was a proud moment for our family. I think we all saw for the first time how the Jewish community had grown in Palo Alto since Mama and Papa had first arrived.

Weddings, Bris and Bar Mitzvahs

Family gatherings of a religious nature also occurred for bris (circumcisions), bar mitzvahs and weddings. As a young child, I looked forward to the party we had for a bris, whether for my younger brothers, or for friends and family! It often took place at our home when a baby boy was a week old. A mohel would come from San Francisco to our home to perform the duty. Richard was circumcised later because he was a "preemie". As usual, Mama and my older sisters cooked for the event. Uncle Ellis, Aunt Annie and friends would come. Papa and the other men often went outside for a drink and a smoke, and we younger kids ran around celebrating. The recipe that follows was Mama's favorite drink for special occasions, such as a bris or bar mitzvah.

*****

Cherry Vishnik

For each sterilized, wide mouthed quart-jar, add the following:

2 cups fresh, ripe bing cherries
1 cup sugar
vodka or brandy

Fill the balance of the jar with vodka or brandy. Cover and let stand 6 months in a cool, dark place.

*****

As for bar mitzvahs, my brother David never was interested in studying for a bar mitzvah. Irving, who always was interested in learning, took the train once a week to San Jose for religious training, and eventually had his bar mitzvah in the synagogue there. Once there were enough Jewish families in the area, Mr. Blackman, who was well versed in the Torah, taught all the boys of the Beth Jacob founding families their bar mitzvah. Richard was one of the first to have his bar mitzvah at the Blackman's home in Menlo Park, and Sydney, in time, had his in the Beth Jacob synagogue. In those days, the rite of manhood was a much more modest affair than the full-blown bar mitzvah extravaganzas of today. In fact, in those days it was mostly just the men who attended a bar mitzvah. After the ceremony, the men would have a drink (schnapps or Mama's cherry vishnik) and a piece of pickled herring.

Bas mitzvahs, to celebrate the coming of age of young women, were not even part of our consciousness. As for confirmations, Jeanette and Sid Gutterman were the first of the founder's children to be confirmed at Beth Jacob. They walked down the aisle of the synagogue, side by side, to the pulpit. Sid, who was a dreadful tease as a teen, kept making asides to Jeanette that it was like they were getting married. She, of course, was very serious about the service and, while pretending not to hear the asides (and not so quietly telling him to "shush"), was quite solemn. It was amusing to watch the performance! And when it was time for the next generation, my daughter Susan was in the first confirmation class at Beth Am.

Esther with Sam Edelstein (taken at the Ranch)

Elaine and Ben Jacobson (taken at the Ranch)

Last, but hardly the least, weddings were, and still are, a big event in our family. I remember many weddings, but especially that of my oldest sister Esther; she was a beautiful bride, tall and elegant. It was in 1924, and the wedding was held at the Cardinal Hotel in Palo Alto, which was the newest and finest building in town. The hotel had a beautiful staircase (which is still there as I write), and Esther walked down those stairs to the main lobby. She just radiated, she looked so lovely. She was marrying Ben Jacobson, who was six foot two or more. I wouldn't call him handsome, but he was good-looking, and had a good sense of humor.

After Esther and Ben married, they moved to Watsonville where Ben had a job with his brother and then, later, he went to work for the police department. They had one child, Jack, who was born in 1925, and who died in the summer of 2001.

Sadly, several years after Jack's birth, they divorced, and Esther moved back to Palo Alto, where she lived and worked until her death in 1990.

I especially remember this wedding because I was one of the attendants. I was 15, fat, awkward, and wore the most ugly horn-rimmed glasses. I remember Mama squeezing me into a corset to make my dress fit. She was disgusted with me, because whatever she tried to do, I just looked terrible, and apparently I wasn't very cooperative. I don't remember much about the actual wedding ceremony, except that Esther walked down the staircase at the hotel, and that there was a dinner afterward, but I was too self conscious to remember or enjoy much.

My sister Elaine married when she was 19. Actually, she was the first of my two older sisters to be married. I remember that it was a big deal because she had gone to San Francisco and bought a very expensive beaded dress, and really wanted her wedding to be special. Mama was very pregnant with Sydney at the time, and I can still hear Elaine giving Mama hell for being pregnant. "It's a disgrace," I can remember her yelling. We kids ran for cover when Elaine started yelling, so I can't tell you what Mama said back to her. The wedding was held at our Emerson home. It was a nice, big, family wedding—Uncle and Auntie came, Mama cooked up a storm, and Papa gave Elaine away. Elaine, who married several times, first married Les Silverstein of Gilroy. He was half Jewish. They lived in Gilroy, and he opened a dress shop. After Elaine divorced Les, he was killed in an automobile accident.

The rest of us got married when we lived on Channing Avenue, and these special events are highlighted in that chapter. However, I want to mention my brother Irving's marriage to Yetta Haber in 1927. Irving was attending Stanford when he met Yetta. He was extremely smart, and my parents hoped that he would be the first of their children to graduate from a university. Sometime in his first year, Irving met Yetta. He was fond of saying that meeting Yetta was like being hit with a bolt of lightning, and they soon made plans to get married. I chaperoned them in 1926, just after I graduated from high school, on a trip to Yosemite Park. The all-year highway to the park had just opened, and the trip was a big adventure for all three of us. We saw the Sequoias for the first time, gawked at Bridal Falls, which were roaring from the late spring rains, and viewed Half Dome in the moonlight. There were even some of the last of the California Indians still living in the park, and we got to see them living as they always had. We pitched a tent, and, let me tell you, we also just about froze to death during the first night in cold, mountain weather because we

Irving and Yetta in Yosemite, 1926   *Irving and Yetta's wedding photo*

were so poorly equipped. (We resorted to stuffing newspapers in our clothes to try and keep warm). Fortunately fellow campers took pity on us and helped us out.

The following year, Yetta's family had a big wedding for the couple in the Witcomb Hotel in San Francisco, which (at the time) I thought was very sophisticated. There was a lovely wedding ceremony, and, after, there was a very fancy sit-down dinner, and I am certain it was kosher because Yetta's mother was very traditional. For me, it was a nostalgic evening, and I remember thinking how special the wedding seemed, and how happy they looked.

Oh, one last thing. An important staple of all Levin holiday celebrations—especially weddings—was Mama's chicken liver. Flavorful, surrounded by fresh rye bread, or crisps, on a platter, it is delicious. Even my son, who is a vegetarian, ordered Grandma's chicken liver to be served at his wedding in 2002!

*****

Chopped Chicken Liver

1 lb. fresh chicken livers, washed and cleaned (do not buy frozen livers)
1 or 2 hard-boiled eggs
1 large onion, chopped
salt and pepper
rendered chicken fat
Best Foods mayonnaise

Clean all the livers carefully to make sure there is no trace of green bile on any of them. Fry livers in chicken fat or vegetable oil until done. Do not overcook. Drain.

Using a clean pan, slowly saute the onion in fat or oil until golden. Cool.

Grind liver, onion, and egg. Mix with chicken fat and mayonnaise to taste. Refrigerate.

*****

While Mama's chicken liver was always the starter, it was the celebration of family, shared faith, and determination to build a better life for ourselves and others, that shaped our family. As I look at our grandchildren and great-grandchildren, it seems to me that we are blessed that these values continue to be alive and well in the extended Levin family.

Emerson Street

What University Avenue looked like when I was a child, about 1914 (Palo Alto Historical Association)

Shortly after Mama and Papa paid off the mortgage on Homer Street, they bought a slightly larger house at 913 Emerson Street, and we moved there in either 1916 or 1917. Although Papa had already moved much of the junkyard, our family moved on my birthday, but I'm not sure if I was seven or eight years old.

To set the context of our family's story during the eight years we lived on Emerson, the nation was undergoing significant change: automobiles became the norm for transportation, telephones were in use for communication, radios became popular and the weekly newsreels brought events in Europe to young and old alike.

Like the nation as a whole, Palo Alto also changed and, at the same time, experienced its first growth spurt during the first quarter of the twentieth century.

When my parents moved to Palo Alto, there were less than 2,000 residents; in 1909, when I was born, there were 4,000; and by 1920 there were 6,000. In those days, the town boasted three restaurants: two Chinese and, my favorite, Sticky Wilson's (it was located on the corner of University and High). Sticky Wilson's was a hangout for Stanford students, and was essentially a restaurant and candy store—which was why it was my favorite. In addition to the restaurants, there were at least two bakeries, one located on Hamilton Avenue and the other, Thompson's, on Homer, that specialized in bread. There was also the University Creamery, next door to the Stanford Theater, that did a good business in sodas for the movie crowd, and, of course, there was the Peninsula Creamery, which delivered milk and cream to its customers each day. The Peninsula Creamery still is in the same location, on the corner of Hamilton and Emerson, and still is very popular, but it is no longer owned by the original family. And, while they still serve great milkshakes, you sure can't get them for a dime.

In the late teens, of the 20th century, Palo Alto was booming. It had also had two women's clothing stores—a big department store, Fraser's, where Esther eventually worked, and Mendenhall's, which was not as large, but stocked lovely clothes. There was Tom Christy's shop, which specialized in children's clothes, and Wideman's, which sold men's wear and offered hand-tailored suits. There were two pharmacies, one located at University and High, and Weingarten's, where we did business, in the same block as the Stanford Theater on University. There were two shoe stores, Thoit Brothers and Farrell's. There also were a couple of shoe-repair shops which, not surprisingly, our large family frequented. A Greek man owned one, and he had a black shoe-shine man who worked on the street in front of the shop for years. He was very friendly and well liked—at least we kids sure liked him, and he knew all our names. I also remember Congdon and Crome (still in business) which sold stationery supplies, and Werry Electric, rounding out those merchants I remember from our childhood in Palo Alto.

As for social meeting places, one was located on top of the old Post Office, at the corner of Emerson and Hamilton. It was a big hall, run by the Native Sons of the Golden West. It was used for meetings and dances. There also was an Elk's Club, located on top of the University Avenue Pharmacy and, eventually, the Mason's Hall was built on the corner of Florence and University. Earlier, when we lived on Homer Avenue, the Woman's Club, on the corner of Cowper and Homer, was built. At the time, it was considered a big, modern building, and we kids used to walk there and watch the construction. (It was later the scene of Dorie's musical performance.) As for children, there was the library, which used to be located where the City Hall is now sited on Hamilton Avenue, across the street from where, years later, Fred's and my store, Henriques Interiors, used to be (now University Art).

Finally, there were two movie theaters: Stanford Theater and The Varsity, both located on University Avenue. From the time I was a young child, the theaters would change movies on Saturdays, and it was always our big thrill to go to the movies once a week. I think it cost a nickel to see a movie until just before the Depression. Years later, during the Depression, the movie theaters had a gimmick to draw customers—a cash draw where the winner would get a percentage of the take. Of course, we used to go every week with the hope that maybe we would win. Actually, Richard's name was called one week, but he had decided not to come that day because he was tired and dirty after working, and didn't want to change clothes. It just about broke his heart to think he wasn't there to get his winnings.

It was in this vibrant and growing community that my parents optimistically believed our family would continue to grow and prosper. Papa traded in the horses, and now drove a truck for his business. We even got a new car—a Model T Ford—that had to be hand-cranked to start. It was black (the only choice of color), and had a canvas roof and plastic windows (but no wipers) that could be attached when it rained.

Mama was pleased with our new home. It was located on the southeast corner of Channing and Emerson Streets, about four blocks from University Avenue or "downtown". Originally, the site was the old federal telegraph property, and it was where Mr. Lee DeForest, frequently called the father of radio, invented the first electronic tube. The lot was 100 feet by 150 feet, and one of the features my parents considered an asset to the property was that there was a large factory building at the back of the lot, in addition to the well-built house. I am certain my folks purchased the property for the location, which was more centrally located than our place on Homer, and, because it was across the street from the Dudfield Lumber Company, a

913 Emerson St. and Palo Alto Junk Yard (formerly site of de Forest lab)
(Palo Alto Historical Association)

large prosperous business of the time. Thus, Mr. De Forest's old factory became the new Palo Alto Junkyard. All of this is gone now. All that is left is a California Historical Landmark #836 marking where our home (and Mr. DeForest's) formerly stood.

At the time we lived on Emerson, the area was an exciting place to be for a child. Because our new lot was larger, my folks also bought and sold secondhand furniture, machinery, old pipes and other assorted materials, as well as sacks and bottles—anything Papa could sell. And I do mean, anything. One time, shortly after we moved to Emerson, he came home with a load of bones to sell for fertilizer in San Francisco. The stench was terrible, but he said we had to live with it overnight. We sure were miserable, but Mama made sure that Papa was miserable that night, too. He never brought home bones again.

We kids all thought the house on Emerson was quite modern, because it already had electricity, and it had finished, white, wood siding. There were two bedrooms with a bath between them. The second toilet was off the back porch. There was a formal parlor, a large dining room with a coal stove, and a kitchen with a wood stove, a small gas heater for hot water, and a large cabinet that held flour, sugar and dishes. Before we actually moved into the Emerson Street house, Dad built a large sleeping porch off the back porch, that accommodated six of us. We each had one drawer for our clothes, and we all shared one closet.

Richard, the baby, initially slept in Mama's room. Once Jeanette was born, she slept with Mama, and Richard was moved into Papa's bedroom. I guess that was their form of birth control. Dorie now slept with the rest of us kids. Poor Dorie—because she was younger than the rest of us, she had to go to bed, in the dark, on the cold sleeping porch earlier than everybody else. She still remembers that David and I would scare her into silence by telling her stories about the Boogie Man, and telling her that if she told Mama, the Boogie Man would come and get her, and sell her to the gypsies.

A few years later, when the older girls needed more privacy, Papa built a wall in the sleeping porch to separate the girls and the boys. Again, as we did on Homer Avenue, we all shared double beds. In the wintertime, I remember, it was a race from our warm beds on the cold sleeping porch to the dining room, to get dressed in the warmth of the coal stove. And I can still remember dodging the sacks of coal and kindling, on the back porch, in my rush to the back door.

The house also had a basement with a dirt floor. Mama had shelves built into it to store apples, root vegetables, her kosher dill pickles and homemade sauerkraut, which she put in big stone crocks. Oh, by the way, remember the family's dill pickles? ("Who could forget?" says my favorite son-in-law). Mama would put up about 200 jars of pickles every year to give away. Everybody loved those pickles and wanted her secret recipe, and, eventually, even Mama's Japanese gardener had her pickle recipe. It was only at the end of her life that she stopped making pickles, and then told me that she didn't even like pickles, but put them up because the family seemed to like them. This tradition still is carried on by many of the women, and even some of the men, in our family, who can't resist a lug of small cukes and the boiling kettle in the middle of the summer. The recipe that follows is adapted from Mama's recipe for today's smaller portions, but the processing remains the same.

*****

Levin Family Kosher Dills

Mama always instructed us to only buy the freshest of small pickling cukes, #1 size, for the crunchiest little pickles.

For one quart of pickles
About 15 to 20 #1 size cucumbers
5 cloves garlic
small head of fresh dill, including the stalk
1 teaspoon pickling spices
1/2 bay leaf
1/2 red pepper
1 rounded tablespoon non-iodized salt
boiling water

Scrub the cucumbers. Sterilize one-quart jars and lids before starting to can. Clean several heads of garlic, and have the spices and fresh dill-stalks handy. Have boiling water ready.

For each quart, fill half the jar with cucumbers, standing them upright. Add 3 cloves of the garlic, the dill and pickling spices, then fill jar with more pickles. Add the rest of the garlic and the salt.

Fill jars with boiling water to 1/4 inch from top. Seal and tighten lids. Turn upside down for 1 hour. When cool, place in dark, cool, storage area. Pickles will be ready after three weeks, although some family members can only wait two! Note: In her later years, when Mama lived on the corner of Cowper and Oregon, she would refrigerate her pickles in order to have them last longer.

*****

Shortly after we moved to Emerson, my parents acquired a swing-glider, and soon it was installed on the front porch, where it became a fixture in our lives. It was especially valued by Elaine and Esther during their World War I courtships, a few years later. A large palm tree shaded the front porch, and there were beautiful pepper trees in the row between the sidewalk and the street. There was also a wonderful cherry tree on the side of the house. We had a battle with the birds each year—they loved the cherries, too.

Although we all worked, while growing up on Homer, it seemed like there was more time for play then. By the time we moved to Emerson, everyone had their chores to do, and there wasn't much playtime. Of course, Elaine and Esther kept their eyes on the younger ones for Mama, but they also washed the dishes each night and helped Mama with the cooking. Esther was like a mother hen—each night she would put rags in Dorie's beautiful blond hair to make curls, and, every morning, she would comb them out before she left for work. We younger ones had to help as soon

as we could. On Homer, when David and Irving were old enough, they used to feed the chickens, pigeons and rabbits. On Emerson Street, each day after school, they sorted metal in the junkyard for Dad. They would sort out the brass from the copper things so we could sell the various metals separately, because we could get more money for sorted metals. I think they also helped out in the Yard on Saturdays. The boys never were expected to help in the house.

My chores on Homer followed a similar pattern to my brothers': I initially gathered the eggs, swept the kitchen, and eventually, watched the babies as I got older. When we first moved to Emerson, and I was eight, my main job was to wheel the younger children around to entertain them. Mama used to say, "Louisa, take them to get air." Actually, I think it was my mother's way of getting me out of the house and from underfoot. I can remember one incident from that time while I was in charge of watching Richard. He was a darling, sweet child, but he had neither the desire nor will to fight. He was always

Richard at age 2

very creative and loving. As a result, I was always egging him on to try to get him to fight, and stand up for himself. I don't remember what the dispute was about, but I do remember Mama coming out of the house and, believe me, I really caught hell for trying to teach him to be a pugilist. That was the end of Richard's boxing and my coaching career. In a few years, Richard didn't need my coaching anyway. He had started in business. I think his first job (at around six years old) was selling *The Saturday Evening Post* on University Avenue.

Notwithstanding my coaching aspirations, my other responsibilities grew as I grew—like those of my older brothers and sisters. By the time I was ten, I did most of the shopping for the family. I used to ride my bike to get some of the groceries and meat from the market for my mother. We shopped for meat at the Stanford Meat Market (located on Ramona between University and Hamilton), which later was the first site of Henriques Interiors. For groceries, there was Earl and Company, and Fuller and Company—both stores had home delivery and also catered to the estates in Atherton.

Years later, we started shopping for groceries at Liddicoats, a store located on University Avenue. It was an open-door market, had sawdust on the floor, and was known in the town for its fresh produce and meats. They had four butchers who would cut the meat to your order, and a conveyor belt from the butchers to the cashier, who would wrap the meat and take the money. I remember that I did not trust the butcher, and would insist on going into the cold storage to pick out the meat for the family. I don't remember why I initially didn't trust the butcher, but when I was about 13, he put his arm around me, so I quit going into the cold room with him.

Lars Larson ran the delicatessen and sold groceries at Liddicoats. He was the father of Virginia, who eventually married my brother, Sydney, and also of an older daughter, Helen, who was my school friend. Lars' store was called a groceteria, and it was one of the first self-service grocery stores. Prior to that, customers were always waited on by clerks. Lars, who was Danish, specialized in homemade potato salads and cold cuts. Because I shopped for the family, I would go to the groceteria, visit with Helen, get the usual full load of groceries and meat, and ride home on my bike. One time, I decided to show off, and rode home with "no hands". Unfortunately, I wasn't looking ahead, and hit a big ditch where the town was putting in a new sewer line, and I flipped over, and the groceries scattered all over the place. I never did that stunt again, but occasionally, I would take ten cents of the grocery money and sneak a root-beer float at the University Creamery. Eventually, somebody who worked at the Creamery told my sister Elaine (always the family boss) about my visits to the Creamery, and I never did that again, either.

I can also remember taking the younger children to buy shoes around that time. I considered it an important responsibility, and took this job very seriously. Years later, the owner of the shoe-store, Ed Zwierlein, told me that I wouldn't take his word that the shoes fit, and insisted on feeling where the toes came on the new shoes. I guess Mama must have impressed on me the importance of careful shopping, and the need to check the accuracy of something before a purchase. I do remember that she always bought us shoes at least a size larger than we needed, so we could get our money's worth.

Around the time I was starting to shop for the family, I also got the job of hanging out the wash. At least once a week, Mama would send out our clothes to be washed at the Stanford Laundry, located on Forest and Ramona. Most of the laundries would have someone come to the house to pick up the dirty clothes, and at the end of the day, they would deliver clean, "damp dry", wash. Washing machines and dryers were not yet invented, and wringer-washers were still too expensive a purchase for our family. Thus, the laundry service saved Mama both time and her knuckles. Although we couldn't afford it, in the early 1920s, the Stanford Laundry employed at least 10 women who just ironed shirts. I used to watch in envy at the thought of getting my brothers' shirts ironed by someone else.

Because the clothes would come back "damp" (wet), and it was my job to hang them out on the line, the next day, I had to take them in. Soon, I also had the job of ironing. I would come home after school and start ironing, take time out for dinner and studies, and then go back to ironing until late at night (or at least it seemed that way). And, remember, Mama always insisted we had clean clothes at school, so there was a lot of ironing. I became very good at ironing my brothers' shirts. Later on, because I was good at mathematics, my jobs changed, and Papa and I would review his eccentric record-keeping, send out bills and, together, we would write the charges into his ledger. At the time, neither of us knew what a debit or credit was, but somehow, he and I managed to collect what was owed. Fortunately, business was mostly done in cash and not on credit, as it is today.

In addition to the Stanford Laundry, there were also two Chinese laundries in Palo Alto that Mama occasionally would use. One of these families' names was Jew. Like our family, they had a bunch of children, some of whom were childhood friends with Richard and Dorie, but it was always a bit startling for our family to hear about the Chinese Jews. Mrs. Jew was a bit of a Palo Alto legend, and a lot like Mama—always there for a person in need.

As is mentioned in another chapter, the fish man stopped at our house on Fridays. Mama was a good customer of his. With all the mouths in our family to feed, Mama always bargained for the best price for the best piece. I think it was a game between the fish man and Mama to see who won each week. The ice man also delivered on Fridays, which was helpful because of the fresh fish which Mama would ice immediately. When it was hot, we kids would follow the ice truck, and when the ice man cut the ice for customers, sometimes we'd be lucky and get the shavings. Most of all, I remember the vegetable man who came twice a week. He had a diamond in one of his front teeth, that sparkled when he smiled. We kids were so impressed by the tooth, but Mama said it was because he didn't brush his teeth.

Mock Sam was a Chinese farmer who sold us vegetables and, over the years, became friendly with our family. He would often come to the Yard, and bring lychee nuts and other Chinese goodies for us kids. We always looked forward to his visits and, at Chinese New Year, he would bring all of us presents and candied ginger. Mock Sam called me "Gimme a Nickel", and would tease me a lot. I must have asked him for a nickel at one time, but I don't remember doing so. He used to pull my hair as he sat around and talked to my dad. Besides Mock Sam, we were neighborly with a Chinese family who lived about a block from where we lived. They owned one of the Chinese restaurants in town. Every year, around Chinese New Year, they would string a clothesline out in their front yard and hang bacon on the line to dry. Occasionally, our dog Prince helped himself to a slab of bacon—like Papa, he didn't keep kosher, either.

A bittersweet memory from around that time also involved our dog Prince. We always had a dog as kids. I guess Papa thought it was a good idea to have a guard-dog for the junkyard, but most of our dogs could hardly be called upon to protect anything except their food. Poor Prince: he had a habit of stealing the lunches of the workmen at the lumberyard across the street. We kids thought it was funny, but they did not. This went on for at least a year. One worker must have put poison in his lunch bag, and Prince was poisoned, and died. He was such a pretty collie and, needless to say, we were a bunch of very unhappy kids.

Of course, our lives were not all work. My father came home one day with a huge collection of toys for us kids, after a call on a very generous Atherton millionaire. This man's children were grown, and when he heard about all the children of Jake Levin the Junk Man, he gave Papa all his children's old toys. We were given a lion, life-sized and covered with lion fur, and mounted on four wheels so we could pull it. It also had a handle just below the neck, and when we pulled the handle, the lion would roar. Another toy was a life-sized pony, covered with real horsehair. I remember that the pony was self-propelled with bicycle pedals, and its hooves were positioned to look as though it was galloping.

We also got a huge wooden horse that was stationary, but would rock back and forth. We put this on the side of the house, right behind the cherry tree, and every child in the neighborhood would come to ride the wooden horse. We must have been an amusing sight when we paraded our zoo on the sidewalk—custom-made toys for the junk man's children. We played with those toys for years, and sure enjoyed them. I have never seen anything to compare with their uniqueness.

By the time we moved to Emerson Street, all of us kids had friends and, of course, there were our cousins. Henry, Uncle Ellis' and Aunt Annie's son, often came on Sundays, and we kids would head off to see the local baseball games. I adored Henry because he always bought us ice-cream cones, and was so much fun to be around. There was an Italian family named Betini who lived next door. The father was a cement worker, and they became good friends to the family. The Fortune family, who lived near us on the corner of Emerson and Addison, also became family friends. They had the most beautiful lilac bushes in front of the Emerson Street side of their house, but, like so many things in old Palo Alto, the house has been enlarged and renovated several times, and the lilacs are long gone. The good thing is that the house is still there!

My brothers and the Fortune boys had a secret fort in the large yard at the Fortune home. They even had a tunnel leading to the empty lot next door, and they had an underground clubhouse. Girls were absolutely forbidden (me included!), and the boys spent hours underground. As we got older, one of the brothers became a bit of a local hero. He had built one of the first crystal sets in town, and always listened to the baseball games. As a result, he knew the scores before they were published in the Palo Alto Times. He was known to take a bet on a score and, guess what, he always won. Nobody in town seemed to catch on.

The youngest girl in the Fortune family, Vera, was the same age as Dorie. They became good friends, and would often stage dramatic events for all the kids in the neighborhood. One time, Vera and Dorie decided to put on the show "Twin Beds" for the folks and our neighbors. They had seen the movie and became determined to put on the play. For the time, the movie was considered risqué and a bit off-color, although the two girls didn't realize it. Richard was pressed into service; he was assigned the role of the leading man. I was assigned the role of "business manager". I can't remember what I was supposed to manage, but we made flyers and insisted that everybody in the neighborhood be there. We charged admission, sold lemonade and other refreshments. After the production was all over, Mama was furious with Dorie, shook her finger and said it was a "shanda", a disgrace, that we kids had put on. She said we had shamed the family, and was embarrassed. We just thought the play was funny, and had no idea it had a lot to do with sex.

Julia, Jacob, Dorie and Richard (taken at Alum Rock Park)

World War One

World War One started in 1914, with the United States entering in 1917, and although I don't remember very much, because I was five when it started, the war eventually made a significant difference in our life as a family.

Initially in Palo Alto, there was a big thrust to help the Belgians, who were faced with starvation. Women's groups were called upon to knit, and to roll bandages. The headlines in the papers called the Germans "Huns", and there was a lot of fear mongering. There was much talk and anti-German feeling among the press and the public. In fact, there was a nice German family, the Kaisers, in Palo Alto who changed their name to Somner, because of the intense anti-German feelings of their neighbors.

My parents were very troubled by the warmongering, as well as by the fact that there was no word from Papa's family, despite their repeated efforts to contact them. We all anxiously waited for the newspaper each day. Once it arrived, my brother Irving would read about the events in Europe to Mama and the rest of us. It was never good. Notwithstanding the grim news, our growing family continued to take priority.

Papa worked all the time, and because of the war, and because there was a shortage of raw materials, prices of scrap metal went up quickly. Overnight, he made a considerable amount of money because metal or iron was worth so much more. As important as making money was, Dad was a man of his word, as well as a businessman. For example, one time, he had committed to a price for some kind of metal. In the interim, the price went up significantly, but he kept to the deal he made on his handshake, even though he could have got a couple of thousand dollars more for it. I remember the incident, because he made the point to us kids that "you

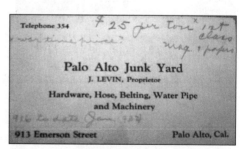

Papa's business card (Palo Alto Historical Association)

should keep your word." He believed, and acted on the premise, that you didn't have to sign your name. One's word was as good as the law. In fact, I remember Dad saying, "When you die, all you leave is a good name, or a bad one."

My brothers Irving and David learned that lesson the hard way. One evening they were playing cards, and one called the other a cheat. Papa overheard this exchange, took away the cards and tore them up. He said, "If this is what happens when you play cards, there will be no more card-playing in this house." And there wasn't. This is probably the reason that none of my brothers ever seriously gambled (at cards, that is).

During this time, when Esther turned 16 and Elaine turned 14, they began to ask to go to dances with the young soldiers who were stationed nearby. The soldiers at Camp Fremont were seen as a bonanza by my two older sisters: boys, and more boys. Although Palo Alto was a very safe place—girls could walk anywhere at any time of day and not be afraid—Mama insisted on chaperoning them to be sure everything was under control, so occasionally she would take the girls to the dances and, of course, she was pregnant. We all knew that Elaine really liked the boys, and was a big flirt. Unfortunately for her, the Levin girls were not allowed to go out with or date a gentile, but she did get to dance. And there were lots of lonely soldiers to dance with in the area.

Esther and Elaine, early 1920's

Camp Fremont, one of the large training camps for young draftees, was located on El Camino Real, and went all the way from the San Fransquito Creek to Santa Cruz Avenue, in what is now called Menlo Park. These young soldiers were all over the area. They dug trenches in the Stanford hills similar to those in Europe, and held target practice.

I can remember hearing the sounds of the artillery practice. By times, they also marched down the streets of Palo Alto to cheering crowds.

In 1918, there was a serious flu epidemic that hit all of the United States, including Palo Alto. Schools were closed, and we kids were kept at home. Merchants were asked to wear gauze masks to prevent germs from spreading, but still many people died; I think more than 30 soldiers at Camp Fremont died as a result of that flu. Fortunately, none in our family was seriously ill—Mama made sure her kinder were kept at home during the highly contagious period.

It seemed like all the Jewish soldiers stationed at Camp Fremont eventually found our family. Our home became the informal Jewish Service Center for the soldiers. Mama always had extra

WWI Soldiers parade on University Avenue in 1918 during flu epidemic with gauze masks (Palo Alto Historical Association)

people for dinner, and would be sure to give them food to take away. Papa had found a wind-up Victrola and a few records—Caruso, and a Jewish Cantor who sang religious and Yiddish songs. Mama loved this music, and played it often for our guests. However, it was the piano, which had become part of our family on Homer, that now had new life in the parlor on Emerson. Esther knew all the popular songs of the day. At night, all the soldiers would come to our house, and Esther would play the piano, and they would sing and sometimes dance. We younger kids weren't allowed to be in the room, but we would sneak down from the sleeping porch, and peek at the oldest ones having fun. One of the songs we always got a kick out of was called "KKKKKatie", which we sang each day on the way to school. Not surprisingly, Papa soon became disenchanted with all the extra soldiers around. Because he worked such long hours, he liked to go to bed early, and

Elaine at 16   *Esther at 16—18*

soon he was complaining that he couldn't sleep with all the noise. Not that it did any good with a house full of kids.

I am certain that Mama kept her eyes on the girls at all times, but, even with her vigilant supervision, Elaine met a young man named Les Silverstein. His father was Jewish, and his mother was not. They had a hot romance, and wanted to get married in fairly short order. Their wedding, and those of my sister Esther and brother Irving, are described in another chapter.

As for my older sister Esther, when she finished school, she immediately got a job as a salesgirl, selling fabrics and notions for Fraser and Company, a big department store located on University and Emerson Streets. The store had a basement and a mezzanine, and it was very modern for the time. Esther was much more the homebody than Elaine, and was shy with the soldiers, except when she played the piano. There was a very nice Jewish soldier, Phil Reece, who had a real case on Esther. He was wonderful—at least we all liked him—but she didn't like him because he wasn't tall enough, and she said he didn't excite her. Dorie and I both remember the night Esther sat us down, and said that she was determined that her husband would be tall and handsome. But we younger kids were impressed because Phil Reece was such a nice guy and, moreover, he bought a wristwatch for Esther for her birthday—a novelty in those days. After the war, ever the entrepreneur, Phil opened a dry-cleaning shop in Palo Alto, and eventually had a chain of stores that offered bargain-rate cleaning. Elaine eventually ran one of his larger outlets in San Francisco and, as a teenager, Dorie worked at the smaller store in Palo Alto.

During the early stages of the first world war, Mama got pregnant again, but she had a miscarriage. Shortly after that, she got pregnant yet again, and in 1919, my youngest sister, and the eighth child, Jeanette, was born. She was born with a red birthmark on her forehead, and Mama insisted that it was because she had burnt her hands during the fire we had on Homer. None of us could ever figure out the relationship between the cause and the effect, but fortunately, the birth mark faded before my sister was a year old, and the matter was dropped.

Jeanette was a wonderful child. She was bright and cheerful. From the time she was a very young child, she wanted to help. Mama always said it was just part of her nature, which rings true, because as an adult she was always there to help anyone in the family who was in distress. One of my earliest memories of Jeanette is of her, at less than age three, insisting on shucking fresh peas and putting them in a strainer, determined that she was going to cook them to help Mama. Another part of Jeanette's charm was that she was a chatterbox. She wasn't a tattle-tale or a gossip, but she always had a desire to share all the news. Thus, anybody who talked to Jeanette knew everything there was to know about the family. We used to tease her, and called her " The Palo Alto Times" or "The Levin Family Press".

Jeanette, posing at 6 months

Prohibition

Over the years, Papa developed friendships with a number of men through his business. One was a soldier named Boris Kashkit. He was a Russian, and he liked to drink beer with my Dad on the front porch. They often laughed, but because they spoke in Russian, I never understood what they were talking about. There was also Dr. Thomas Williams, who was a Major Surgeon during World War I in the military. He was always interested in antique brass and copper, and Papa always kept an eye out for valuable pieces for Dr. Williams, who would inevitably purchase them. I am sure a couple of Mama's deliveries were paid for that way. Actually Dr. Williams, as an offshoot of his office, along

Jeanette in her Little Rascal's phase, around age 3

with Dr. Russell Lee and Dr. "Fritz" Wroth, started the Palo Alto Medical Clinic. As for Dr. Lee, he was a great chess-player, and I have fond memories of him playing chess on our front porch with our uncle Jack Edelstein, when he visited from Chicago.

In addition to Papa's business friends, there were a couple of characters that came into our lives during Prohibition. The first was Dan Connally, who was an alcoholic. I think he was a concrete worker, and occasionally Papa would hire him at the yard. Dan was as strong as an ox, but he had a hernia which came down to his knees—we kids said it looked like he had an extra body-part there. Poor Dan, he was such a drunk that, during this time, he resorted to drinking wood alcohol, and I doubt that he lasted long after that. Yet another lost soul that became part of our lives was Isaac (at least, that is what Mama called him). He started begging at our door while we lived on Homer, and followed us to Emerson. He had a running conversation with himself constantly. Over the years, Mama would feed him, and have him sweep the yard and do other minor work. However, he always disappeared when Papa had a trainload of scrap to haul.

The other person who came into our lives, just as we moved from Homer to Emerson, and played an important role in our family, especially after Papa died, was Jim Brown, the Yankee. Jim came from an educated family in the east, and had come west to have more room. He could operate heavy equipment, and I think Papa once said that Jim had run one of the first steamrollers used to pave roads. Over the years, he helped Papa in the Yard, and became, by default, an extension to our family. After Papa and Irving died, Jim did all he could to help Yetta when she was running the business. He also was the person who taught Sydney how to drive a car. Of course, they would go to one of the local establishments (Kelly's), and have a couple of beers. In his later years, my brothers hired him as a night-watchman for their business in San Jose. He worked for the boys almost until he died. Jim had no use for his own family, and often said that his children would fight over his possessions before he was cold in the grave. And they did!

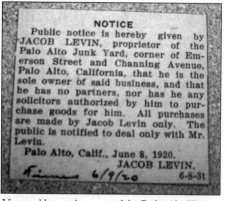

NOTICE

Public notice is hereby given by JACOB LEVIN, proprietor of the Palo Alto Junk Yard, corner of Emerson Street and Channing Avenue, Palo Alto, California, that he is the sole owner of said business, and that he has no partners, nor has he any solicitors authorized by him to purchase goods for him. All purchases are made by Jacob Levin only. The public is notified to deal only with Mr. Levin.

Palo Alto, Calif., June 8, 1920.
JACOB LEVIN.
6/9/20   6-8-3t

You could never be too careful...,Palo Alto Times (Palo Alto Historical Association)

Given my parents' friendships, it was not surprising that when the 18th Amendment to the Constitution—the Volstead Act (Prohibition)—came into effect in 1920, Papa decided he would make wine with some of his Italian men friends. Some guys he knew had access to red grapes, and the wine was to be claret. It was not very successful; it tasted more like vinegar than wine. However, Papa figured out that he could make a profit, and also get good wine, if he sold empty bottles to some of the bootleggers who worked out of Half Moon Bay. He did a roaring business selling bottles to the rum runners (bootleggers), who put fancy labels on any kind of liquor, and, as Papa said, "There was nothing illegal in selling bottles."

During this period when the junk business was booming, my parents bought "The Ranch", which has its own chapter of family stories. It was also during this time that Mama convinced Papa to buy the empty lot across the street from us, and expand the junkyard. After much family debate, my parents purchased the lot on the northeast corner of Channing and Emerson Streets. The Levin family now owned the northeast and southeast corners for the expanding Palo Alto Junkyard. In fact, my brother Richard started what eventually became Levin Metals Corporation (LMC) by selling used burlap sacks in the shed on the new lot. And, while the family "empire" was expanding, Mama was expanding too. She was pregnant again.

On July 21, 1923, Sydney, the youngest of our nine was born. He was the only one of us who was delivered in the hospital, and it was a good thing too, because he

was over nine pounds when he was born. Dr. Edith Johnson was the attending physician. In those days, the hospital was located on Embarcadero Street, which is now the site of the Lawn Bowling grounds. Syd was a beautiful baby, and he was such a well-behaved child—well, almost always.

Mama holding baby Sydney, Jerome Edelstein looking on at left

The Levin Ranch

From the time I was a young child, my family enjoyed picnics and outings in the country. This tradition continues today with the Levin Family Picnics, including the family discussions before, during, and after, of what there is to eat for lunch. As with most children, when I was growing up, any kind of trip was a big event-especially one with a bunch of kids, a pregnant wife and a rickety truck. And, of course, over the years, we had many adventures on our way to and from family picnics.

For Papa, his favorite recreation (especially as a younger man) was to go to the Russian Baths in San Francisco when he had a load of junk to take to the City. He would always stay overnight, drink with his friends, have a couple of steam baths, and return home refreshed. Mama never took a vacation. She stayed home, and took care of the family and junk-

Mama with me on her first vacation, late 1930's

yard until I took her on her first trip to Los Angeles, and to San Diego to visit friends in the late 1930s.

For our family, Alum Rock Park was the favorite place to have fun and to picnic. It was known for its mineral waters and was a favorite of our parents, my aunt and uncle and, of course, for all of us kids. It might have reminded the adults of some of the Russian spas they must have seen when they were young. For us, it was just fun.

The spa was relatively simple. There was a central watering hole in a circular area, similar to an old bandstand, with four faucets surrounding a center structure. People would line up and help themselves to the different types of waters, sulfur water being the most popular. The park also had a large aviary with many colorful birds, but the main attraction for us kids was the large covered swimming pool. It had a large slide similar to the popular waterslides of today, and only the good swimmers were allowed to go on the slide.

Several trips to Alum Rock Park stick out as especially memorable, particularly because they set the stage for my parents to look for a country retreat closer to home. The first occurred when I must have been around six or seven. School was about to start, and this was to be our last trip until the following summer.

Mama got us up at dawn to pack up a super picnic lunch. We put on our best clothes and were checked to see if we were spotless. We left soon after in our truck. Six children from the ages of 14 to two sat on boxes that were placed on the bed of the truck. Richard, the baby, was in front with Mama and Papa.

What is important to keep in mind are two things. Firstly, Dad was the worst driver I have ever known. He sure knew how to handle horses and a wagon, but a car or a truck was a different matter, especially one full of kids. He drove at one speed—slow—and this tended to extend our traveling time. Thus, although it sounds as if we traveled great distances for our family picnics, it is only 20 miles from Palo Alto to San Jose.

Secondly, before 1940, all travelers heading north/south between San Francisco and San Jose used El Camino Real, built along the old Spanish missionary trail. Also, when I was a child, El Camino Real was a two-lane country highway, and not even paved all the way. In fact, some of the poorest roads were found in Mayfield, just south of Palo Alto. There were potholes about one foot deep in some parts of the road. (Bayshore Freeway did not exist until much later; it was all salt marshes and orchards until the 1960s.)

As for our end-of-summer-family-picnic, we left home and drove south, passing through the dusty streets of Mayfield and eventually, but slowly, passing Mountain View and Sunnyvale. This was our favorite part of the trip because on both sides of the highway—for miles and miles—all one could see were apricot and prune orchards, with an occasional small vegetable farm for variation. It is hard to imagine this landscape now in the South Peninsula, but it seems only yesterday that the aroma from the spring blossoms during the early evening was more heavenly than the most expensive perfume!

We finally came to Santa Clara and passed the old Spanish Mission. After the Mission, we crept by Santa Clara University. In those days, the college was directly across the street from a tannery. The odors from the tannery were horrible. I want to hold my nose now just thinking about those ripe hides. I often have wondered how those students could study, and if they became immune to the aromas arising from the tannery. Smell or no smell, my father continued to drive very slowly. We soon passed through the small city of San Jose (the population was then about 50,000) and eventually started climbing the foothills toward the park. We got halfway up the incline when the truck stalled. Papa became rattled, and could not restart the truck. All six of us children had to get out of the truck and help push it up the hill. Mama, who had a new baby on her lap, also had to get off and help push. It was hard work (coupled with lots of Russian swear words from Papa, and asides from Mama), but finally the truck started, and we all piled into the back again and headed to the park.

Another endless driving trip I took with Papa was for one of his business trips to Santa Cruz. We drove south on El Camino, and then turned onto what is now Highway 17. In the early 1920s, Highway 17 followed the creek beds over the Coast Mountain Range, and was a narrow, winding, often dirt, road with no place to pass. Dad drove so slowly that cars were backed up for what seemed like miles and miles. I think Papa was driving our Model T Ford, and it overheated and stalled, which made matters even worse. I remember other drivers yelling a Papa when they finally were able to pass. People had road rage even in those days!

However slow and entertaining the trips were to Alum Rock Park, the end of these family adventures occurred when my two older sisters, Elaine and Esther, traveled to Alum Rock Park with Charles Drabkin, a Stanford student (Jewish, of course) in his new car. Charles was an extremely religious Jew, and all the poor man could eat at our house were eggs, and possibly fish. However, he was charming and

Cousins, probably 1923
Back row: Bobby Levin,
Jerome Edelstein, my sister
Dorie
Front row: Harold Edelstein
and my brother Richard and
sister Jeanette

my parents liked him. Unfortunately, he was a novice driver, and accidentally drove the car over an embankment on the way up the mountain to Alum Rock Park. Charles escaped without a scratch, but Esther had a large gash in her arm and Elaine broke her collarbone. The car was a complete wreck, and they all were very lucky they were not more severely hurt. Probably, they were saved because cars were not built to go as fast as they do now. An interesting postscript to this event is that Charles became a doctor, and remained friends with the family.

With all this as background, it was not surprising that around 1920, Dad, who was tired of driving the family to Alum Rock Park for picnics and worrying about his older children in cars, purchased three and a half acres in what was then called "Stanford Weekend Acres", just off Alpine Road, near Bishop Lane, just behind the Stanford Campus. The property faced on San Fransquito Creek, which gave us clean cold water, and also had a small dam in it, above which was a natural swimming pool. At the time Papa purchased the property, it was basically untouched. The land was covered with beautiful oak trees, and in the spring, the green hillsides seemed endless. As a teen, I can remember my delight walking in the grass, marveling at flowers, and listening to the many birds. What I didn't know was that the soil was rocky and poor, which was why there were such terrific grassy hillsides.

Papa and my brothers immediately built a horseshoe pit and marked out a baseball diamond. Believe me, over the years, there were many hot contests and bets taken. Papa especially loved the Ranch, and spent as much time as he could there, particularly in the summer months. He and Uncle often spent time there together, which I am certain was a special treat for the brothers.

On the weekends, friends and our family came together, particularly on hot summer days; to swim and to relax. One

Mama and Sydney

time, somebody must have borrowed my Dad's swimming suit, because he took a gunnysack, put a hole in the top for his neck, sewed up part of the bottom and tied it around him for swimming trunks. We all laughed and cheered! Papa seemed like he could do anything in those days.

Initially we camped on the property, and I can remember that lizards crawled all over us at night and we could often hear the coyotes in the distance calling to each other. Papa soon built a one-room cabin, and immediately installed a wood cook stove for Mama. A couple of years later, because my two older sisters were starting to date and Mama always liked to know where her children were, Papa made sure the ranch was a fun place to come for young adults. He built a spectacular outdoor dance floor—it even had a line of Doric columns along the front that Papa had bought from an Atherton estate. He found an old upright piano and brought it in on

Ellis and Jacob, 1929 (the brothers enjoyed their time together at the Ranch)

Papa (in the burlap bathing suit) with Jeanette, 1922

the back of the truck with great ceremony, for Esther to play, and even recycled our old wind-up Victrola for music.

One Sunday, shortly after Papa had built the dance floor, and when there was a big crowd at the ranch, Irving and David caught some fish in the creek and paraded them around for one and all to admire. They eventually put them in a bucket, and put the bucket in the shade until it was time to fry them up. Richard, who was about eight years old, Gerry Marcus and Harold Edelstein (who were both six) were very impressed with the fishing prowess of my older brothers. They kept playing around the bucket, and peeking at the fish. Richard wondered how the fish would act if they all peed on them. Not well, it turned out, because the fish swam around the bucket like they were trying to escape. The fish were eventually cooked and served, but the boys refused to taste them, and giggled like crazies as the adults all admired the taste of the fresh fish!

Unfortunately, Dad also had aspirations of becoming a weekend farmer and having bountiful fruit trees, much like those that covered the hillsides farther along Alpine Road. In short order, he cut down most of the oak trees and planted an orchard of young trees. A couple of

My first date with Fred at the Ranch, 1932 (note the Doric columns)

years later, ever mindful of saving a dollar, Dad decided to prune the fruit trees (not knowing a thing about pruning trees) to ensure a bountiful harvest. What a sick bunch of trees they turned out to be! For a few years, we got some fruit, but the harvest was never bountiful. To make matters worse, a few years later, Richard and David bought some steers and put them to graze at the ranch because it was fenced. Obviously, the steers ate what fruit there was, and soon stripped the trees bare. That

*The Naughty Boys: Back row: Gerry Marcus,
Richard Levin, Harold Edelstein
Front row: Jerome Edelstein, Sydney Levin*

ended Dad's endeavors with fruit trees, and, to make matters worse, most of the beautiful oaks were long gone, too.

Notwithstanding Papa's efforts to civilize the Ranch, all our friends from San Francisco to San Jose would come to see us in the "country". Every Sunday, a crowd would gather, and Mama, who I never saw in a bathing suit, would feed them all. Whether just for friends, or for the many fundraisers my parents hosted for Beth Jacob and Jewish Youth Groups, Mama would make tubs of potato salad and her famous beans, and other great food. It was the Levin's Free Lunch. As I look at it from the perspective of my parents, I think they were so happy to have a place close to home for their children and friends. The older folks would sit under one of the few remaining oak trees near the cabin, and visit with each other. My brothers, sisters and I ate, danced, swam, and, as we got older, we smoozed with friends who came to visit.

Years later, Papa and my younger brothers Richard and Sydney enclosed the dance-floor to make it a recreational hall. Richard hauled large stones from the creek and they built a magnificent rock fireplace. Papa had saved some of the mosaic work from the old Stanford Chapel destroyed in the 1906 earthquake, and Richard used these bits to trim the rock fireplace. It was quite artistic. Not surprisingly, as they grew older, all my brothers used the ranch as a place to take the girlfriends. Sid Gutterman told me that, as a pre-teen, he made the mistake of walking into the cabin one weekend, and being cuffed by Richard and told to butt out. At the time, he was quite put out, as he didn't understand what was going on behind the closed door. Another time, Mama, who had not been to the ranch for a while, found the cabin and pavilion quite dirty. She was furious, and told them they should be ashamed of themselves because the sheets were so dirty. My brothers just laughed and teased her, saying they had received no complaints!

Some years later, when Papa was sick during the Depression, Mama (who was worried about bringing in income) decided to rent the dance pavilion to a Stanford fraternity for a party. It must have been a drinking fraternity—remember, it was also during Prohibition—and the students got really drunk on illegal gin, and heaved all over the building. The building stunk for weeks after, and Mama, who loved the Ranch almost as much as Papa, said that while the money may have been good, the smell wasn't worth it.

As the saying goes, all good things must pass, and so did the Ranch. We kids grew up, married, and moved away. By 1937, Papa and Irving had died, and Mama (who never drove) had no way of getting to the Ranch even if she wanted to. Yet Mama was reluctant to sell it. Because I was still living at home and working at the bank, I

Levin cousins picnic, Boulder Creek, 1995 (The Mishpucah love to eat!)

bought half of it to keep the property in the family. Mama kept the other half for Sydney, who had spent many happy hours there as a teen, and loved the ranch as much as Papa. Once Syd came back from the war, and married Virginia, they moved to San Jose in 1945 to join Richard and David in business. Not surprisingly, he needed instant cash to buy in with the boys, and so we sold the Ranch.

On spring days, as I drive past the endless suburbs which surround Palo Alto, and head past the big buildings which now clutter the Stanford campus toward Alpine Road, I can still see some of the wild things in the surrounding foothills, but they are becoming harder to find. Today, there are new suburbs of large, very expensive houses off Alpine Road near Bishop Lane. Yet the Ranch still lives: all three of my brothers purchased property in Boulder Creek, and as a result, our children and grandchildren have had the opportunity to experience the perfection of morning in the country, smell the redwoods, feel the intense heat of the day, as well as run, swim, ride horses, have a game of softball with their cousins, and catch crawdads in the creek. And, as my brothers, sisters and I have aged, our family still gathers, by times, for those wonderful family picnics!

333 Channing Avenue

333 Channing Ave.

"Thank God you were born in America"

In the 1920s, Papa's business was very successful, and prospects were even better. Feeling confident my parents, in 1924, decided to buy this beautiful, large family home at 333 Channing Avenue. Papa went with pride to the bank to get a mortgage for our new house. When he came home, he told us that he had said to the banker that it wasn't a bad house for a junk man. The banker said, in return, that it wasn't a bad house for a banker. Thus, it was with these high expectations that our family moved from Emerson to Channing.

Mama and Papa, 1929

And the house was beautiful, as was the property it was built on. First of all, the block was lined with mature acacia trees which were absolutely gorgeous in the spring, although my sister Dorie had a terrible allergy attack each spring when they were in bloom. The property was 100 by 200 feet, which for a family home, in town, seemed large enough for us to do everything we wanted to with a home. Three beautiful California live-oak trees graced the house site, along with a plum tree, an apple tree, two walnut trees, a quince, a persimmon tree, and a fig tree just outside the back porch. It also was located close to the junkyard, which was very convenient because Mama could still walk to the junkyard and help out with sales during the day.

The house itself was a very spacious two-story home. Upstairs, there were four bedrooms, two of which had walk-in closets and built-in dressers. Of course, there was the usual large sleeping porch, and a large attic where Mama stored walnuts over the winter (one year, the squirrels got in, and the crop immediately vanished!). Downstairs, there was a spacious living room with a fireplace, a dining room, a large kitchen, a pantry and a screened-in back porch. There was a basement with a dirt floor, and shelves for storing pickles, jams and other preserves. (It also had cobwebs and spooky spiders, according to some of the grandchildren). And, for the first time in our lives, we had central heat from the oil furnace in the basement. What luxury!

Because our life in the Channing Avenue house spanned more than 30 years, it is difficult to do justice to the things that happened around us, and to us, in a short book such as this. For example, as a family we experienced the exciting growth of the 1920s. In fact, it was during the 1920s that, as we kids became young adults, we got the traveling bug to see the wider world—the Russian River, Yosemite National Park (which, in 1926, had just opened year-round), the Grand Canyon (Uncle Ellis and I visited there in 1936. I rode a donkey to the bottom and back!) and, in 1933, the Chicago World's Fair! It seems strange to speak of our 1920s perception of travel—with my son now living in Brazil, my daughter in Canada, my granddaughter studying in London, and grandson in New York City—but, for those of us who grew up with a horse and buggy, travel by car to exotic natural wonders was the wider world.

As we all know, the 1920s ended with a thud and the election of cautious, conservative Herbert Hoover (whose home was at Stanford) as President of the United States. Subsequently, the 1930s brought the Great Depression, and hard times for many in the United States. There were breadlines in Palo Alto and hobos lived in the San Fransquito Creek, but we were fortunate because everyone had a job during the worst of the Depression. However, our family was not immune from its effects. Only one of us children was able to go to college, and the pressure on my father to maintain his business and look after our family led to what today would probably be called severe depression.

In the 1940s, World War II brought fear to us all, with the wholesale slaughter of European Jews and the seeming indifference of the rest of the world. It also brought us food and fuel rationing, and the forced internment of Japanese-Americans all along the west coast of the United States. Every day, there was bad news—the European Continent was controlled by the Nazis, and most of South-East Asia was overrun by the Japanese. And while the rest of the world was engaged, the United States remained neutral. Then Pearl Harbor was bombed and, although we did not have the instant visual images that we did with September 11, 2001, everyone's life changed and the country prepared for war.

Sydney joined the Navy to fight the Japanese in the Pacific, while David and Richard were exempted from the service because they were running an essential wartime business. Fortunately, my brothers-in-law Ted Smolen and Rubin Lewon were also exempted because of their professions, and my husband, Fred, who worked in a defense plant, was considered 4F (unacceptable) because he had flat feet.

Following the war, we watched as veterans flocked to the west to complete their education under the GI Bill of Rights. Not surprisingly, because of the open space in northern California, clean air, good water and wonderful climate, they soon bought homes in the region using low-interest loans. Indeed, fueled by these loans, the whole of California grew and changed, and by the 1950s Palo Alto extended well past Oregon Avenue to the south, and east to Bayshore Highway. Our family had changed, too: by the 1950s, all of us nine children had married, Papa and Irving had died, and most of the grandchildren had been born. Thus, over the 30 years that the Levins occupied the Channing house, we had our share of happy times and sad events.

Early Adventures on Channing

Because business was booming in the early 1920s, around the same time as we moved to Channing, Papa bought some wonderful furniture at a "good price" from an Atherton millionaire. If I remember correctly, these items had been shipped from England to San Francisco, around the Horn on a clipper ship, and were then carted by horse to this family in Atherton. The furniture was magnificent. There were several different kinds of mahogany chairs with expensive upholstery, lion faces on the armrests and paws on the bottom. There was a large buffet and also a stand-up two-sided mahogany mirror. The dining room table was an especially handsome heavy mahogany piece: in fact as I write this I realize now what a gorgeous thing it was. It was an oval table that opened up to seat over 20 people for special occasions. We all loved that table, and it was the place of many delicious meals and family discussions. Foolishly, I refused to take it when Mama eventually sold the Channing Street house, because Fred and I preferred modern furniture at the time.

Sydney, as I mentioned earlier, was still quite young when we moved to Channing Street. As with most young boys, he would occasionally get into mischief trying to emulate his two older brothers. He must have seen Richard or David carving wood with a knife for some project and, as a result, decided to become a wood-carver too. Because he closely observed his two older brothers he, quite handily, was able to find Dave's straight razor in the bathroom, and climbed underneath the dining room table to start carving the legs. That went so well that he then went on to enhance the door between the front hall and the dining room, and then went on to the buffet. Not surprisingly, Mama soon found out what he was doing.

Sydney knew he was in deep trouble when Mama quickly took him upstairs to the bathroom, and stuffed him in the wicker basket so Papa couldn't find him when he saw what had transpired. Knowing how Mama operated, Papa soon found Syd in the basket and took him downstairs to the kitchen, pulled down his pants, and gave him his first spanking with another of Papa's finds, the cat-of-nine-tails. It was a leather strap cut into about six separate pieces, each about a foot and a half long. The handle was made of wood and leather, and rounded. I don't think Papa used it that much, but Mama used it to threaten us when we misbehaved, saying "If you don't behave, I'll tell Papa." Although it

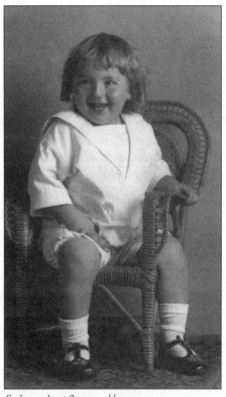

Sydney, about 2 years old

hung as a deterrent in my closet when my children were young, ultimately Sydney inherited the strap and has given it to his son Gary, who now has it mounted above one of his doors. As for Sydney's carving, Mama covered it up with paint and varnish, but that wasn't the end of Sydney's work with the razor. Some years after this carving incident, Syd borrowed David's razor once again to shave; he still sports the scar on his chin.

This last incident brings me to the one constraint in this large luxurious home: it only had one full bathroom, which was located on the second floor. (There also was a toilet downstairs, near the kitchen.). The bathroom was a large room, even by today's standards—about three times as large as is the average bathroom—although there was a lot of wasted space, with just a bathtub and a washbasin. It had a large linen-closet that eventually became a shower. The toilet was in a small adjacent room—almost a closet. Not surprisingly, with a bunch of teenage children and young adults, there were the usual fights over who got the bathroom first.

One incident I remember has since become a family joke: Richard was in high school at the time, and was getting ready for a date. Sydney, who was still young (and idolized his two older brothers, Richard and David), was watching Richard preening before the mirror. Somehow, Richard left the room, and Dorie snuck in, and promptly locked the door with her and Sydney inside. Richard became extremely upset, and started yelling and banging on the door. He was so mad that he broke the lock off the door with his force, turning and twisting the knob. Of course, the door-handle no longer worked from the inside, either, so Dorie and Sydney were stuck in the bathroom on the second floor. Eventually, after much yelling and recriminations between Dorie and Richard, and laughter from the rest of us, Mama made Richard get a ladder and climb through the bathroom window to get Dorie and Sydney out of the room, and then he had to fix the door. We all got a real kick out of the entertainment, but needless to say, Richard was not amused and of course Dorie and he were late for their dates.

Caroline

No story about the Levin family would be complete without mentioning Caroline. She came into our lives around the time we moved to Channing. In the 1920s, the State of California placed people who were wards of the state out in families to do menial work. I think my parents hoped that they could find someone who would relieve Mama of some of the household responsibilities. However, Caroline had limited mental capabilities ("retarded", as we called it in those days), which was why her family made her a ward of the state.

Caroline

Caroline was one of the kindest and most warmhearted persons I have ever known, but she also was one of the most poorly coordinated, as well as having very bad eyesight. This combination was a constant disaster. Many of Mama's favorite dishes were broken within a short time after her arrival—this was long before dishwashers—and I know that on several occasions Mama was ready to send Caroline back. However, it was difficult to stay cross at Caroline because she was always extremely remorseful over any accident, respected Mama, loved the garden and all the children and the grandchildren, and they all loved her back. Eventually, she became one of the family.

One thing I particularly remember about Caroline is that she could keep a secret. Thus, anytime one of us did something we shouldn't have, and said to Caroline not to say anything to Mama, she'd always say back with great emphasis, "Me! NEVER would I would spill the beans out of the pot." Not surprisingly, Caroline knew most of our secrets.

Many years later she used to sit for my children, and Stephen (whom she adored) used to get her to sit by his bed and rub his back for hours. Unfortunately, as an old woman, Caroline got cancer of the liver, and eventually had to go to the County Hospital in San Jose to be properly cared for. All the family would take turns to visit her, and she was always so happy to see any of us. It was a joy to visit her, and remember the good times and laughs we had when we all lived on Channing. The hospital administrator remarked how faithful we were to her; but even as adults, we kids still had a special bond with our Caroline.

My Parents' Friends

Neither of my parents had much leisure time because their first priority was their children, and their second priority was the business.

Yet, over the years, Dad developed a number of men friends through the junk business. My parents also were

Business advertisement for the Junk Yard, Palo Alto Times (Palo Alto Historical Association)

friendly with members of the synagogue, but they didn't entertain or go out for dinner with friends, like we do today. Occasionally, friends would visit us at home, and of course there were Sundays at the Ranch. However one of Papa's friends, who he met during the 1920s, really liked Mama's cooking and visited us frequently. Mr. Kerr was German, and spoke with great affection of "the fatherland", which was not a good idea during World War I, or for that matter World War II. Mr. Kerr always managed to come around dinnertime, and he and Papa would sit on the porch and have a couple of schnapps before, and sometimes after, dinner. Papa said that the first drink made him feel like a new man, and often, of course, the new man had to have a drink, too. Most of the time if he was alone, he only took one. If Mr. Kerr was visiting, they would have schnapps, and a couple of pieces of herring which Mama used to buy by the barrel. It was one of the things we used to eat, boiled herring, fried herring and pickled herring. It was a popular dish in Russia, and Mama said it was a delicacy. I still enjoy the odd piece of pickled herring, which is a legacy from my childhood. I also appreciate oriental art, and I owe that to Mr. Kerr, who was the first person I ever met who had a large collection of oriental art, and who encouraged me to start collecting it.

Coming of Age

While we lived on Channing Avenue, all of us younger kids became teenagers, then young adults and, eventually, married. As a result, there was never a dull moment in our lives. For my sisters and me (because our lives were more supervised), our brothers offered us a window into the larger world. Richard, although a good student, was ever the promoter. He had his backyard development projects (fish pond, waterfall and miniature golf course), his band, his used-burlap-sack business and his girls. He made beer in the basement—one batch exploded during the night, and caused a fright for us all—raised pigeons in the back of the yard and, of course, sold them at a good profit. He also had the "Owls' Club" in the garage—it had girlie pictures on the walls—and poor Sydney was considered too young to be a member. Of course, we girls were never invited in to the "Club".

Sydney, as I mentioned earlier, idolized David and Richard, and followed them everywhere. As he grew, he had his violin, various odd jobs (including plucking chickens, for a short time), his photography and his agricultural projects—from lawn mowing to nursery asistant. Like his older brother Richard, he raised livestock, too—guinea pigs—and sold them for a small profit to a local doctor, who, in turn, sold them (much to Sydney's dismay) at a large profit to Stanford University for research. Also, Syd still maintains that, as the youngest child, he often got the worst of it because the older boys never had to do housework, but he did. Worse yet, every time it was Dorie's job to do the dishes, she had a date, and every time it was Jeanette's job to do the dishes, she'd excuse herself and retreat to the bathroom to read.

My two younger brothers: Richard and Sydney

By the time Dorie and Jeanette graduated from high school, we were in the midst of the Depression. Dorie initially had started college, but quit after a short time to get a full-time job to help the family. As I mentioned in another chapter, she worked for Phil Reese, who ran a chain of dry-cleaning stores and was an early suitor of Esther's. Jeanette (who always claimed that I bought her the first new dress she ever owned) and I were always close, although I was 10 years older. I recommended her for a job in the bank where I worked, and she started immediately after she graduated from high school, in 1937, to help bring in income. This was not surprising, given Jeanette's commitment to the family, and her meticulous organizing skills. Plus, she would never dream of bending a rule—she was the ideal candidate to work in a bank! Even as a teen, Jeanette organized a social Jewish youth group, as well as keeping a calendar on the back of her door with family birthdays and other special events. For as long as I can remember, she was the one person in the family who always made a point of remembering each of us. And she continued to do this until the end of her life.

From my perspective as the older sister it seemed like Dorie, and to a lesser extent Jeanette, dated constantly as well as helping Mama in the house. As with all us daughters, my sisters Jeanette and Dorie were instructed to only date Jewish men, but, because they were younger and times had changed, they were occasionally allowed to go out in a group with "gentiles". If I remember correctly, one of my sisters (I no longer remember who did what) even went so far as to have a couple of secret dates with a non-Jew. My other sister told Mama (ever the psychologist), who didn't acknowledge she knew what was transpiring but instead waited for my first sister to tell her, which she eventually did. On the subject of dates, Jeanette loved to tell a story about the time Dorie had a date with a Stanford student to go to a fraternity dance, but a better prospect appeared on the scene and asked her out for the same night. Because she knew that, at the very least, she was obligated to a find a replacement, Dorie turned to Jeanette (who must have been all of 13 or 14) to take her place on the date with the first young man. Jeanette willingly accepted and went to the dance. While I no longer remember what happened on this date, I do remember that all of this was unbeknownst to Mama, and monitored by Caroline.

As for me, when I graduated high school in 1926 my plan was to work for a couple of years, and then attend university. I immediately found work at the Bank of Palo Alto. I started work at $65 a month, with the assurance that they would give me a raise if I proved to be a satisfactory worker. I was a good worker (I had learned that at home) and after two months, when I didn't get a raise, I asked if my work was satisfactory. Surprised at my audacity, they gave me $20 more a month—$85! Initially, I filed and sorted checks. After that, I was put on a bookkeeping machine, the size of a 21-inch TV on a stand, and a far cry from today's hand-held calculator. A couple of years later, I became one of the first two women bank-tellers in the savings department. However, the bank president decided that the savings department would be ideal training for young men heading toward management, so we were demoted. I was devastated and angry, so I quit.

Fortunately, the president of the Palo Alto National Bank immediately offered me a job, once again as a bookkeeper. I soon was moved to safe-deposit boxes, and then promoted to teller again. I remember getting several raises, too. In fact, I thanked the manager for one raise, and he said to me, "Louise, anytime a corporation gives you a raise, you damn well earned it!" Eventually, I was put in charge of the Bank's loan department. This was as senior as a woman could advance in those days, because the bank had a policy that stated, "All our officers are male college graduates." I was fortunate in some ways to have stayed working, because I worked at the Bank all through the Depression, even during the period in the early 1930s when many banks failed and people all over the country didn't have work.

Actually, because I was making what was considered good money during the Depression, I wanted to do something special for Mama, who always had such a heavy load to carry (and always had many mouths to feed). Thus, shortly after I started work with the Palo Alto National Bank, I bought Mama her first electric refrigerator and I took out a loan to buy it, too. It was so big and heavy I am certain it could have withstood a direct bomb-attack. Mama loved that old upright General Electric refrigerator. She called it "the fridgedairy". She kept it for years, and when she moved to Cowper Street, it became the pickle fridge in the garage. Mama eventually gave it to Beth Jacob for the kitchen and, believe it or not, it lasted until the 1960s, when the synagogue moved to Redwood City.

In the latter part of the 1930s, the Bank once again decided that my position would be a good one to have a male management trainee take over, and I was transferred to become head teller in order to let Charlie Means, the management trainee, take over. But I had my rewards. I was put in charge of the bookkeepers, and seemed to have a knack for immediately finding the occasional accounting error. It used to exasperate the bookkeepers, who were responsible for balancing the books, and, more importantly, the bank had to hire two people to do the work that I had previously done in the loan department. Eventually, Charlie became bank manager, and after Fred and I married he always went out of his way to provide a loan to us at a good rate.

Marriages

As I mentioned previously, Esther and Elaine married while on Emerson. By the time we moved to Channing, Elaine had divorced her first husband, Les Silverstein, and was living in San Francisco. Her second marriage was to Ted Jacobs who managed a shoe-store in Santa Rosa, and then she divorced a second time. By 1933, Elaine was back in San Francisco and sharing an apartment with our cousin, Dora Edelstein Singer.

In 1928, Irving was the first of us to marry while we lived on Channing. (His wedding and photo are described in another chapter.) David then became the next one of us to say, "I do." He had met a young woman who was the daughter of a local furrier, and a real hot tamale. She was attractive, with lovely skin, and a pair of boobs like you never saw in your life. Dave immediately became infatuated, and her parents actively promoted this match as much as they could. So, in late 1928, David, age 20, got married.

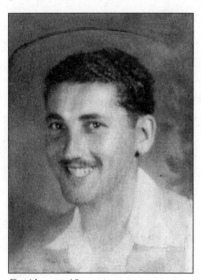

David at age 18.

Some years earlier, Papa had purchased two deep lots on Seale Avenue, near Alma. They were about 200 feet deep, and he built two identical homes, each with five rooms. They shared a common driveway. As usual, Papa tried to get the cheapest prices he could for the materials, so the new homes were built with secondhand lumber and had a floor furnace rather than central heating.

Papa was so pleased to give one of the homes to Irving and Yetta, and the other one to David and his new wife. I think Papa knew he was failing; he was beginning to feel depressed, and was physically not very well but he was so pleased that he could leave something of value to his sons.

Irving, a true Levin, loved to garden and in a short time he and Yetta developed a wonderful yard in their new home. I seem to remember they even had chickens for a time. And, of course, Yetta became pregnant with the twins, Stanley and Alan. They were very happy and we were happy for them. Around the same time, it became evident that Papa was really sick. In fact, within a couple of years, Mama decided to sell the Palo Alto Junkyard to Irving and Yetta, once it was clear that Papa wasn't going to get well enough to work again anytime soon. This was an obvious choice, because Irving was, in effect, already running the business.

It is important to keep in mind that Mama, even while Papa was sick, and while cooking and managing the household for all of us, still helped out in the junkyard almost every day. As I have said previously, she was a great salesperson and she always loved to bargain. She could sell anything. Sydney said that he remembers that it was during this time that she sold a dead rattlesnake to a Stanford student (presumably for a prank). Also, somewhere along the line Mama learned about plumbing. When farmers came in to buy plumbing supplies, Mama knew what they needed, and often provided detailed instructions on how to install the fixtures.

It seemed like events happened very quickly, but it must have been more than a year after David was married that an extremely agitated and angry middle-aged woman stormed up to our door on Channing, with a loaded gun, looking for David's wife. Given all the on-going stress about Papa, this incident was all it took for Mama. That night she had a heart attack and was rushed to the hospital. It was a frightening night after an up-setting day. Shortly after, the marriage was annulled and for-tunately Mama got well, but we all sure had a scare.

Winnie and David, probably 1934

Being young makes you resilient, and David soon recovered from his unhappy marriage. He continued working at the junkyard with Irving, and soon started going out with his pals. During this time, he often went to Lake Tahoe on weekends with his friend Jerry Breit, who played the banjo in the bars by the lake. David didn't play an instrument; he went for the beer, and the girls.

Within two or three years, a Jewish barber he knew set him up on a blind date with a young Jewish girl, Winnie Breslauer, from Chico, who was finishing her degree at Stanford. Winnie was smart, and she was also prudent. Before she came down the stairs in her dorm to meet David for the first time, she had her roommate check him out. I guess David passed, because they soon started dating on a regular basis. He would often take Winnie out for a meal and, although very concerned about showing her a good time, he was careful (because it was during the Depression) not to spend any more money than he had to. As a result, he would always eat a full meal at home before he took Winnie out. I still remember Winnie, who was

David and Winnie, about 1950

small and trim, wondering how she could eat more than David!

It wasn't too long after—in May, 1934—that they went to Nevada, and tied the knot for a long and loving marriage. Dave and Winnie moved to San Jose right after they were married, because David had been offered an opportunity to go into business with Charlie Lerer, who had bought Uncle Ellis' former business on South First Street.

How this business opportunity happened, the story goes, was that as Uncle Ellis

Richard with Mama in the garden: He had just graduated high school

aged my cousin Henry Levin became responsible for his family's business, the San Jose Bottle Works. Unfortunately, Henry wasn't a good businessman. In fact, Henry's main interest was baseball, and it was during this period that he sponsored a semi-pro team. It seems that the players were always short of cash, so Henry let the guys "borrow" petty cash from the business. In time, there wasn't much petty cash, and Henry had to ask a family friend, Charlie Lerer, to help him cover his expenses. It soon became clear that Henry was simply unable to repay the loan. Because Charlie was friendly with Papa and Uncle Ellis, he bought the business with the money he was owed, and encouraged Dave to join him.

David worked long hours to make a go of the business in San Jose. He eventually was able to buy out Charlie Lerer, and shortly after he and Winnie were able to buy their first home, in the Willow Glen region of San Jose. Subsequently, they had two wonderful daughters—Joan, who was born in 1935, and Barbara, born in 1940. In the late 1940s, David and Winnie built a lovely spacious family home in the same area in San Jose.

At this point, I should mention that, in 1933, Richard graduated high school, and was very committed to expanding his used- burlap-sack business. David asked him to join him in San Jose, and, since this was a good opportunity for both my brothers, Richard was pleased to make the move. Initially, when Richard moved to San Jose, he lived in a rented room, but David and Winnie (who had just given birth to Joan) decided that it would be better if Richard lived with them in their new home, which had three bedrooms, and was quite spacious. It came out years later (because David often teased Richard about this), that Winnie had a hard time keeping help and baby sitters when Richard was living with them because he always was after the girls, and was too often successful.

Papa's Depression

One of life's realities is that few of us have all our dreams fulfilled, and most of us sometimes experience great sorrow. For the Levin family, our first major test came when Papa got sick. For years, my dad worked constantly, was always on the lookout for new business, and we prospered. Moreover, Papa was widely respected because everyone knew they could always count on him to keep his word. As I have mentioned previously, Papa believed that keeping your word was the most important thing a person could do in the world, and he often said that a good name was the best thing a man could leave.

Notwithstanding success, Papa was a born worrier. I suspect some of this came from his experiences as a youth in Russia. Thus, when the 1930s Depression hit Palo Alto, revenues at the junkyard fell. Although we always had plenty of food, and could pay most of our bills on time, we were late on some of the mortgage payments to the bank. Owing money, and making late payments worried Dad more than we initially realized. He became increasingly depressed and eventually he could hardly function.

Mama took Dad to several different doctors to try to find out what could be done for him. Sadly, in the 1930s, doctors knew very little about depression, and they said his condition was a result of hardening of the arteries to the brain. The doctors all recommended that we have Dad committed to Agnew, the state mental hospital. Reluctantly, Mama placed him at the hospital, but, after only two weeks, she knew that it was not the proper place for a sick person, and brought him home again. We had a special apartment built off the garage for him, because he was so distressed, and couldn't stand the noise of the remaining five of us kids. Simply eating with the family made him so nervous that Mama had to feed him separately.

To make matters worse, about two years after becoming depressed he developed cancer of the bowel. It seemed like it took a long time to have Papa diagnosed,

Jacob Levin, 57, Called By Death

Jacob Levin, 57, died this morning after an illness of four years. Funeral services will be held tomorrow afternoon at 1:30 o'clock at the Tinney Funeral Home. Burial will take place in San Jose.

Mr. Levin was born in Vilna, at that time a part of Russia, in 1878. He came to California in 1904 and settled in Palo Alto the following year. Since then he has been a dealer in second-hand goods.

Surviving him are his widow, Mrs. Julia Levin; a brother, E. Levin of San Jose, and nine children—Esther Jacobsen of Watsonville, Elaine Jacobs of Santa Rosa, David Levin of San Jose, and Irving, Louise, Dorie, Richard, Jeanette, and Sidney Levin, all of Palo Alto. There are three grandchildren.   OCT 10 1935

Papa's obit. (Palo Alto Historical Association)

but once he was he was immediately put in the hospital and operated on. The interesting thing is that after the operation, and when we thought he might recover, he came out of his depression and told Mama that he was no longer confused or afraid any more. Sadly, he didn't recover and died on October 10, 1935, while still in the hospital. Papa's depression and death left a terrible shadow on our family yet life continued for us kids, now young adults. In fact, Mama encouraged us to have a small New Year's Eve party the year Papa died. She said, "You kids still have to live."

Dorie Marries

Life does go on. All of the family rallied round to help Mama, following Papa's death. Mama rented out the room off the garage, and began to spend more time in her garden. It is interesting to think about Mama's perspective about marriage during this time. She often spoke about the importance of marriage to all her daughters. She also told her daughters, once married, "to keep your husband tired" and "to always look neat at the end of the day to greet your husband". I think she believed that if her daughters followed her instructions, their future husbands would not stray. However, times changed and so did attitudes. Irving's son, Stanley, reports that Mama told him before he married that she thought it wasn't a sin to live together before marriage.

Mama shortly after Papa died

Not surprisingly, in time there were suitors who came to court Mama—the Widow Levin. However, she very clearly said to any potential suitor, "Thank you for the compliment, but I am intent on raising mein children to be good citizens." One suitor suggested marrying her for companionship. She told us that she said, in return, "Companionship, I got mein children."

Life continued for the rest of us, too, even during Papa's illness. Dorie was the next one of us to have a serious suitor, and marry. Sometime in the early 1930s, Dorie met a good looking young man, Ted Smolen, at a party in San Francisco. While Dorie still had a number of suitors, and was actively dating and still interested in several of them, Ted really fell for Dorie, and started coming down as much as possible. He would often take Dorie for dinner and dancing at a place called The Clover Leaf on El Camino Real, where one could also drink and play cards in the back room (remember, it was during Prohibition—this was exciting stuff). We all really liked Ted, especially Mama, who encouraged Dorie to marry him. Thus, shortly before Papa died in 1936, Dorie, at age 23, married Ted. She was a beautiful bride, they were a handsome couple, and it was a beautiful day.

Dorie and Ted had a traditional Jewish Hoopa set up in the back garden on Channing, and Mama cooked up a storm for the party. The whole family turned up, and we had a wonderful time. In fact, my cousin Bobbie Levin (who was married to Craig Taylor by this time but always up for fun) and I got absolutely pie-eyed from celebrating. After the ceremony, Dorie and Ted went to Yosemite Park on their honey-

Dorie and Ted's wedding, 1936

moon, and then set up housekeeping at a rented flat in San Francisco. A couple of years later, their daughter Sandra (Sandy) was born in 1939, and a few years after, in 1942, Joel (Joe), their son, came along. Later on, as Ted's business grew (he started out with a small pharmacy and a liquor license, and expanded the prescription business into servicing the city's hospitals), they were able to build a lovely home in Sea Cliff, a prestigious neighborhood with views of the Bay in San Francisco. Initially, they did a great deal of entertaining, and appeared to have an ideal life. Unfortunately their lives later began to go in different directions as Dorie's health became increasingly affected by depression. In middle age, they sold their home and then separated, but never divorced.

After Dorie married, Syd, Jeanette and I lived with Mama at home. In fact, it was the first time I had a room of my own! Esther moved back the following year with her son Jackie, after divorcing Ben Jacobson. (A year later, she placed Jackie in a

Jack Jacobson while living at Channing

home, near Santa Rosa, that cared for the mentally challenged.) It was during this time that I became serious with my future husband, Fred Henriques. From the time we originally met, in the early 1930s in San Francisco, Fred, who had immigrated to the United States from Jamaica, really pursued me. He told his friends, from the time we first met, "She is going to be my wife." I couldn't believe that this handsome, courtly gentleman, who clicked his heels and kissed my hand, was interested in me. Well, I guess he was—although our romance initially got off to a rocky start because he didn't show up for our first date. He had lost his job, and had no money to come to Palo Alto. However, when he did come down, as I describe in another chapter, my brothers gave him a musical visit never to forget. Fred soon started coming every weekend to hang out with the family at the Ranch. We also used to head to Carmel to stay with a friend of his, whenever we could afford it. It was such a wonderful, sleepy little village in the 1930s, and Fred loved the sea.

Because it was during the worst of the Depression, Fred had a difficult time finding work. In 1934, he decided to return to Jamaica where his family was established, and return to his previous job with the Jamaican government as a surveyor. Fred's family were one of the pioneer merchant families in Jamaica, who supplied all the ships that came to port. I don't know if Fred's father had a partner who gypped him out of his money, or if he gambled it away, but by the time Fred returned to Jamaica, there was no more family money or business.

After a couple of years, Fred returned to the United States with his widowed mother, Julie, and his brother Charles. Fred got a job, selling draperies in the basement of Emporium, and our romance started again, this time in earnest. I must say that I reinforced my future mother-in-law's prejudices of Russian Jews as peasants. One of the first times I met Julie was at a party that Fred had at his flat in San Francisco. He had ordered a keg of beer for everybody to drink up, and sometime during the party, a friend dared me to drink a pitcher of beer. Because I was a beer drinker in those days, and was used to hanging out and drinking with my brothers, I said, "Of course, I can." So, here I was in the kitchen, drinking beer out of a pitcher with all of our friends chanting, "Drink, drink, drink . . .", and in walks Fred's mother, who considered herself descended from European royalty. I must have been a very unpleasant surprise for her, and I know she initially didn't think much of me; although, in later years, she once told me she admired my strength.

More Sorrow

While I was being ro-manced, Irving was running the Palo Alto Junkyard, and David and Richard were doing well in San Jose. Not too long afterwards, Irving started complaining that his stomach was bothering him. He kept working, say-ing that Papa was sick, and he would take time off later. Yetta finally insisted he go see the doctor. The doctor initially thought it was an ulcer, and said that Irving just needed less stress and more rest. I think Jeanette stayed with Yetta during some of this time, helping out at home with the twins,

Irving with Stanley and Alan, 1935

trying to make things easier for Irving and Yetta. Unfortunately, when the doctors finally found out what was really wrong, it was too late. Irving was diagnosed with bowel cancer, and, although they operated, it was a hopeless situation. He passed away in 1937, at the age of 31, leaving Yetta, Stanley and Alan.

Stanley tells a bittersweet story about the day of Irving's funeral. He and Alan didn't go to the service, and stayed at our home on Channing with Caroline. Ever curious, the boys wondered what happened at a funeral, because their only knowledge of death to that point was Halloween. They wondered what their father looked like—was he a skeleton, or what? They wandered over to the adults who had just returned and were sitting on the front porch, and asked if Irving looked like a skeleton. Yetta started to cry. Her mother, Mrs. Haber, scolded Stanley and Alan, and said, "You naughty boys." Mama placed her hands on Mrs. Haber,

Irving I. Levin Taken By Death
JUL 6 '37

After an illness of four months, Irving I. Levin, 31, passed away this morning in the Palo Alto Hospital.

Funeral services will be held tomorrow morning at 10:30 o'clock from the Tinney Funeral Home, followed by interment at the Home of Peace, San Jose.

The deceased, a Palo Alto business man, is survived by his widow, Mrs. Yetta Levin; two sons, Alan and Stanley; his mother, Mrs. Jacob Levin, and the following brothers and sisters: Mrs. Esther Jacobson, Mrs. Elaine Jacobs, Mrs. Louise Henriques, Mrs. Dorie Smolen, David, Richard, Jeannette, and Sidney Levin.

The late Mr. Levin, a native of San Jose, spent practically his entire life in Palo Alto, attending local schools and Stanford University. At the time of his death he was president of Congregation Beth Jacob and the Jewish Center.

Irving's obit. (Palo Alto Times, Palo Alto Historical Association)

and said, "They are only kinder." Knowing they had asked a wrong question, the twins took off, and hid by the hose bib at the side of the house, between some bushes. Syd, who was just turning 14, soon appeared, and walked with the boys, one in each hand, out to the back yard to have a talk and play ball.

Meanwhile, Fred and I had decided to get married. Because Irving was so sick, and Fred and I were scheduled to be married in about a month, we went to speak to the doctor who was treating Irving. He told us to get married immediately. Although we were scheduled to go on our honeymoon later, and Fred and I worked up until the last moment, we got married the following weekend, in the late afternoon on June 26, 1937. Mama and my schoolfriend Helen Larsen made all the arrangements, and did the cooking for the small wedding party. The ceremony was held in the backyard of Channing Street, under the apple tree, which was a beautiful sight next to Richard's pond and also a favorite place of mine. We spent our wedding night at

Louise and Fred on their honeymoon, Victoria, BC, 1937

the La Playa Hotel in Carmel. A month later, we went to Victoria, British Columbia, on our honeymoon. Unfortunately, Irving died on July 5, the day on which we were initially scheduled to be married.

I believe I have mentioned elsewhere that Fred and I originally rented the tiny house in back of the Tyler's home (on Bryant Street near Forrest), which Mr. Tyler had built for Mrs. Tyler—Mama's first American friend. Its rent was $25 a month. Our house, which was more like a cabin, was so small that, even if we could have afforded to buy a refrigerator, it wouldn't have fitted in. There was a tiny icebox, a small stovetop burner for appliances, and we went through a closet to our bedroom, a screened sleeping porch. However, although we were poor by today's standards, our first purchase was a combination phonograph and radio. And every month we bought a new record so that we could start listening to music.

One story I am particularly fond of reminds me of that time. Next door to us was a small apartment house. There was a couple of maiden sisters who lived in one unit. One of the sisters had a parrot that she babied, and the first thing she did every day, when she came home from work, was to take the parrot for a walk. One day, she left the apartment, loudly scolding her pet parrot, "You bad, bad boy, you left my bedroom," (or something like that). Fred and I were outside, and when he heard that, he started to laugh and hooted, "My God, I think she sleeps with that damn bird!" I think the whole neighborhood heard the news.

Notwithstanding my happiness, it was a very sad time for all of us, after Irving died. Mama grieved deeply about Irving, as she did for Papa, but through it all she continued to say, "Thank God you were born in America." Everything was better in America compared to the old country. Never did we hear that the strawberries were better in Russia.

Yetta also grieved deeply, while she tried to carry on at the junkyard. Jim Brown, "the Yankee" who had come into our lives while we lived on Emerson, and who was living at the Ranch during this time, helped out at the junkyard, as did Mama. Syd recently told me that it was Jim Brown who taught him to drive around this time, and that they would drive to the Alpine Inn to drink beer. Although Jim was helping, as did Mama, it became clear that the business was too much for Yetta, who was still coping with the loss of her husband and caring for her two boys. As a result, within a year, she sold the business to Charlie Unger, and moved to San Francisco. A few years later, Charlie moved the business to Mayfield and ran it there until he retired.

When Yetta first moved to San Francisco to get settled, Stanley and Alan (the twins) moved in with Mama on Channing. Because my other brothers no longer lived at home, Mama impressed upon Syd that he was the man of the house because Papa had died. Sydney, who is all of five or six years older than the twins, really looked out for the boys. He took his paternal job extremely seriously, even to the point of occasionally punishing the twins. Stan recently told me that during this time Syd caught the two boys lying, and, like Papa, took them upstairs, took their pants down and whacked them with the cat-of-nine-tails.

Old salvage company changes location AUG 30 '44

"The junk yard" at Channing avenue and Emerson street, landmark for 39 years, passed out of the Palo Alto scene this week when the Palo Alto Salvage and Supply Company moved to its new location at 3001 El Camino Real.

The business was started at the old location by Jake Levin in 1905. It was purchased by Charles Unger, its present owner, in 1939.

The new building, constructed at a cost of $8,000, is located at the corner of Olive street and El Camino Real, where the Southern Pacific railroad crosses the highway to Los Altos. The new plant has a railroad spur which will be used to send salvaged metal directly to plants where it can be put to use building materials of war.

End of the Palo Alto Junk Yard, Palo Alto Times (Palo Alto Historical

But Syd was much more than the "Enforcer"—when the two boys started school at Walter Hayes Elementary (they even had the same teacher as Syd), he was responsible for the twins skipping a half grade because they already knew their times-tables. Most importantly, Syd saw to it that there was always fun for the twins. In fact, he even installed a basketball hoop on the oak tree that was by the driveway in front of the garage, for the three of them to shoot baskets. It was still there, in 1957 when Stan came back to Palo Alto to start up his dental practice. By then the Palo Alto Medical Clinic had taken over the entire block, but for some reason the tree was still standing and the backboard and hoop were still attached.

During this time, Stan and Alan were encouraged to take piano lessons (Mama never gave up her desire for a family musician). Stan still remembers doing duets with Alan, but he said the most fun was listening to Esther play the piano. Their favorite sing along piece was, "Let's all sing like the birdies sing, tweet, tweet, tweet." They loved to tweet with Esther at the piano.

Henriques Interiors

That same year—1938—Fred and I were able to afford a move to our own new home at 310 Addison Street in Palo Alto, across the street from the now-famous garage of Bill Hewlett and David Packard. We paid $35 a month for rent. I hesitate to even consider what such a rental in that neighborhood would cost in today's dollars. When

310 Addison Street

The opening of Henriques Interiors on Hamilton Avenue: Esther, Louise and Fred at left center, 1950's

we moved in, the house was new, and it had no garden. I put in the first garden, and I think some of the original plants are still there. As we both worked on the weekends, Fred and I shared housekeeping. I would go out to weed and mow the lawn, and Fred would change the bed and dust.

Fred always wanted to open a furniture and drapery store, and in 1939 we had our opportunity. By way of luck a small lamp shop, located at 521 Ramona Street (formerly La Piere Market, then Stanford Meat Market), went out of business, and we took over the lease with capital of $1,000 from a note that my mother guaranteed.

I continued to work at the bank for the first two years, and we lived on my salary. Fred worked the night shift at a defense plant during World War II, and his salary and all the profits from the business were re-invested. It was during this time that my sister, Esther, came to work for us at the shop. Once the store was up and running, my first child, Susan, was born in 1942 and then, two years later in 1944, just after we moved to our home on Madrono Street (two blocks south of Palo Alto High School), my son Stephen was born.

After the war, because of the increase in population from all the returning soldiers buying new homes in the area, the business grew. We were soon making custom drapes and upholstery, as well as selling furniture and accessories. By the end of the 1940s, Fred had become very well known in the area for his decorating talent, and for his charm. All the ladies liked him. As a result, he spent most of his time designing the interiors of homes, and soon was catering to the expensive Atherton and Woodside clientele. Esther and the others on staff sold at the store. Initially, I kept the books in the office and did the advertising, but ultimately we needed a full-time bookkeeper. Thus, by the early 1950s, we were able to expand, and moved around the corner to Hamilton Avenue, where University Art is now located. The business continued to grow, and Fred was asked to teach interior design for the Palo Alto Adult Education program.

The Levins Grow, Again

While Richard was working with David in San Jose, and was still living with David and Winnie, he became friendly with Arthur Lackman, who told him that he had a younger sister who was going to University of California at Berkeley. At the time, Richard was going out with a couple of girls in San Jose, but Arthur arranged for an introduc-

Jeanette, Sydney with Richard and Emmy at their wedding in the garden, 1939

Richard, Emmy, Dorie and Ted with kids, 1945

tion. Soon after, Richard brought Emmy Lou to meet the family. She was so pretty, charming and sweet that we all instantly fell in love with her. Needless to say, his sisters encouraged Richard to grab Emmy before somebody else did. A year or so later, on May 14, 1939, they tied the knot and they, too, had their marriage ceremony under the apple tree in the backyard at Channing. It was a small family wedding, and Emmy's two brothers gave her away. They were the first of us to sail to Alaska—they went on a freighter for their honeymoon.

Meanwhile, David and Richard had been working very long hours to build up Uncle Ellis' business again. However, they didn't feel the business could grow much more in the existing location on South First Street because, in part, they were still renting the site from Auntie. Around this time, Richard and Emmy decided to invest her small inheritance in the business to help it expand. As a result, the boys were able to buy property on South First (now called the Monterey Highway), which, at that time, was the main thoroughfare south to Gilroy. They constructed an all-purpose building, and developed a bigger yard to expand the business, which eventually became Levin Metals Corporation (LMC). And, to make the circle complete, a few years later, cousin Henry was asked to come to work for my brothers at the new yard. My brothers always said that Henry was a good worker, but a terrible entrepreneur.

While the boys were building the business, Richard and Emmy started building their family. They eventually had three daughters: Elsie, who was born in 1940, Beverly, who was born in 1942 (and who died in 1992) and Janice, who was born in

1949. Their first home was in Willow Glen and, shortly before Janice was born, they purchased quite a bit of land in the East Foothills of San Jose, which, in the late 1940s, was still country. Subsequently, Richard developed a number of lots, built a couple of houses for resale, and, as well, he and Emmy built a large family home with a fantastic view of San Jose. An interesting sidebar to this development project is that Elaine and her third husband, Ted Kay, lived for a number of years in one of the homes that Richard had built. During this period Elaine, who was a fantastic cook, ran a very successful catering company.

Uncle Ellis

Uncle Ellis while at Channing, 1945

Families are always interesting, sometimes too much so. In the early 1940s, Auntie and Uncle must have had a doozy of a fight. I believe Uncle had become increasingly concerned that Auntie was giving too much money to Cousin Henry who, in turn, was still not investing it wisely. As a result, Auntie got so mad that she kicked Uncle out of their home, and they divided their property. It was a difficult time for the entire family. Uncle and Auntie's kids trod lightly so as to not further alienate either of their parents, especially their mother. Thus, Uncle moved into a rooming house in San Jose, rather than compromise any of his children. All of our Palo Alto family adored Uncle, and felt very badly about what had happened, but didn't feel we could intervene. However, because Richard was living in San Jose, he made a point to see him as often as possible. Richard felt badly about Uncle Ellis, and became increasingly concerned about his living conditions. Thus, he asked Mama to let Uncle Ellis use his room, and live at

Channing instead of the rooming house in San Jose. Of course, Mama agreed and Uncle Ellis came to stay on Channing for a time. Given the always delicate relations between Mama and Auntie, Uncle's move created family tension, especially after Auntie accused Mama and Uncle of having an affair, although nothing could have been further from the truth.

Uncle was happy staying with Mama on Channing. He often brought her to visit me just after I had given birth to Stephen, and he took Mama shopping and for drives out back behind Stanford. That being said, he missed his children dearly. Well, time passed, and injuries healed. After a couple of years or so, Uncle eventually moved back to live with Auntie in San Jose. He died in 1949, and she lived until 1958.

The Last Two Get Married

In the late 1930s, the Jewish community was still quite small in the Bay Area. Our family knew almost everybody who was Jewish, because of our involvement with Temple Beth Jacob. New residents always were made welcome, and were often invited to join us for Sundays at the Ranch. This was the case for the Lewon family, recently arrived from Montana. One son, Rubin, had a great personality, and was a chemist who worked at an asbestos plant in Redwood City. Once my sister Jeanette and he met, they fell in love. Jeanette said it was a match made in heaven, so after an intense courtship and short engagement, they decided to marry in May of 1940. It was a small wedding, and it was held in the living room at Channing. My sister Elaine and I were already scheduled to take a cruise to Alaska, and thus missed the wedding.

Initially, Rubin and Jeanette lived in Palo Alto. In fact, at one time, they lived next door to Fred and me on Madrono Street. Rubin and Jeanette had two of their three children while living in Palo Alto. Carol was born in 1941 and Robert (Bob) in 1942. Shortly after Bob was born, Rubin was transferred, and their family moved to Orinda, in the East Bay, for several years. Sometime after World War II ended, Rubin (who had been working for an industry considered an essential occupation by the military) was able to consider other business options. He and his brother, Louis,

Dorie with Jeanette and Rubin at their wedding, May 1940

Elaine and Louise on Alaska trip, May, 1940

Fred and Louise, Rubin and Jeanette in Carmel, 1940

started a salvage business in San Francisco and the family moved there soon after. Their third child, Jeanne Louise, was born there in 1948.

Also, when World War II ended in 1945, Sydney returned home from the Navy.

Esther, Mama, Susan (who was about two years old), and I (with my infant son) were there to meet him when he arrived at Channing. We were all so excited to have Sydney safely back with us—after all, so many sons and daughters had been lost, not to mention the millions of people of Europe and

Lt. Syd, home from World War II

Susie, always gardening, by Richard's pond, 1943

Asia. Susan says that one of her first memories is of her uncle coming across the lawn, laughing, swinging her in the air, and then giving her a stuffed Koala bear.

Sometime in the next few months, Esther held a luncheon in the back yard at Channing for the Palo Alto Business Women's Association. Virginia Larson, the younger sister of my friend Helen, attended. Syd, fresh from his time in the Navy, met her that day and immediately started to take her out. In short order, they were married. The ceremony took place at Jeanette's and Rubin's home in Orinda. It is interesting to note that they were the first of the extended Levin family to be married by Rabbi Gitin, who was a young rabbi practicing in Berkeley and a friend of Jeanette and Rubin. Subsequently Rabbi Gitin became the rabbi at Temple Emanuel El in San Jose, and I have lost count of how many of my nieces, nephews and the next generation he has married. He has also buried a lot of us, too.

Around the same time, Richard and David invited Sydney to buy into the business in San Jose. Because David had received the house on Seale Avenue as a wedding present, and Mama had helped Richard when he joined David in the business, she and I agreed to sell the Ranch and she gave Sydney half of the funds from the sale. Initially, Sydney and Virginia rented a small home in the development that Richard had built below his home in the Foothills of San Jose. They eventually purchased a family home near David in the Willow Glen neighborhood. Virginia gave birth to Gary in 1948, and the last of Mama's grandchildren, Virginia (Ginny) Kathleen, was born in 1950.

With most of her children now living elsewhere, Mama sold the corner on Emerson and Channing where the Palo Alto Junkyard was located. She rented the second lot across the street to the Palo Alto Co-op, which put a gas station there for a number of years. Today, there is an auto-repair business on the site. Although the business has been long gone, it is comforting to know that the Palo Alto Historical Association still has a copy of Papa's business card in their files, and a record of his original purchase of the property on Homer Avenue.

Sydney and Virginia, 1945

As for the Channing Avenue house, in 1951 Mama sold it to the Palo Alto Medical Clinic, which, at the time, was located behind our home and in the process of expanding. They bought our home for $30,000 and used it for several years as a research centre. Eventually, they bulldozed it down for a parking lot. Today, the block on Channing is once again in transition and a large condominium complex is being built on the site of our old family home. I think for each unit you can probably add a zero to the $30,000 Mama received for the entire property.

Julia's Last Home

Mama in front of her rhododendrons at Cowper and Oregon

Mama was tired by the time she moved to the house on Cowper and Oregon. In fact, the main reason she agreed to move from the Channing Avenue home was that her heart doctor told her she could no longer take the stairs, or manage the large home and garden, because of the stress to her heart. Esther was still living with Mama at the time, and so they made the move together.

The new house was located on the northwest corner of Cowper and Oregon, which, in the early 1950s, was almost the southern border of Palo Alto . The home was a modified ranch-style house, and considerably smaller than the Channing Avenue home, and, most importantly, it was on one floor. Mama quickly planted a number of rhododendrons in the front yard, and for a few years, had a small vegetable garden in part of the back yard, where she grew tomatoes and cucumbers for pickles to fill the "fridgedairy" in the garage. Esther had a Steinway baby grand piano in the living room, which she enjoyed playing in the evening and on weekends. Eventually, Mama put her television in the living room, too.

Shortly after, Mama moved to Cowper and Oregon, one of my brothers got her a parakeet for a pet so that she wouldn't be lonely. She doted on that bird, and trained it to say a few words. The best part was that the bird spoke with a Russian accent, and had many of Mama's mannerisms. She also taught it to eat from her mouth, and play cards, frequently telling us that the bird was a good pinochle player. The bird used to sit on her shoulder and that of her helper, Cedolia. One day, Cedolia went outside with the bird on her shoulder, and that was the last time the bird was seen.

The new home was farther away from town, and Esther, who had previously never driven a car, now needed to do so. Initially, she resisted, saying that she and Mama could take the bus to town to shop. Esther was still working for us at Henriques Interiors, and found it easy to ride the bus to work. The rest of us lobbied for Esther to learn to drive, but, of course, we also helped by shopping for them, and taking Mama to the doctor. Others helped drive, as well. Family friends, the Shockers, were very fond of Mama, and, because they lived quite close, used to drive her each week to Beth Jacob for services. Finally, Esther agreed to take driving lessons because Fred convinced her she needed to for work. She had an awful time learning how to drive, and took lessons for what seemed like an unreasonable amount of time, but, she finally got her license, although she refused to ever drive on the freeway.

It was a good thing that Esther learned to drive, because Mama lived almost another 20 years on Cowper and Oregon, and, during that time, the town changed considerably. For example, in the 1950s, the area south of Oregon Avenue was annexed to the city, and thousands of new single-family contemporary homes were built by Joseph Eichler, and new elementary and junior high schools—and even another high school—were built. The Stanford Industrial Park was developed just north of El Camino, making Oregon Avenue (which previously was a relatively quiet thoroughfare) the major thoroughfare into its southern end. Town and Country Village (across from Palo Alto High School) and the Stanford Shopping Center were created, and many of the larger retail shops moved to these new sites from downtown. Late in the decade, the same pro-growth movement also produced more development on university lands (such as the Stanford Hospital Complex) and behind Stanford (creating Portola Valley and Foothills College). Over-development reigned, and, as a result, the pace and style of life in Palo Alto changed fundamentally. The car was king, along with its ugly side effects—traffic, the need for more roads because of congestion, and the beginnings of smog in the Santa Clara Valley.

The Pickle Lady

In the midst of all this change, Mama seemed an island of calm, and she continued to cook for one and all. We bought her a big freezer so she could keep baking, and my brothers built shelves in the garage to store pickles, her jams (raspberry was her favorite, which she called roseberry) and other canned foods. Mama became well known in the family and among our friends and their friends for her pickles and, over time, became known as the Pickle Lady. Her doctor, William Clark, probably gave her this title when he told his children, who loved her pickles, that they came from the Pickle Lady. They lived nearby, pointing out Mama's house to their friends, and word spread rapidly among friends and family alike. Jackie Lehman, the daughter of our family friend Jeanne Lehman, still remembers biking over to the Pickle Lady's house with her friends after school because she knew they would always be well fed. Rabbi Teitelbaum (the Rabbi of Beth Jacob at the time) also used to visit Mama on a regular basis with his young family, who enjoyed being so well fed.

Although Mama became known for her pickles, I can't remember a time when Mama didn't have baked goods, at least some mandelbrot and Rice Krispies squares, hidden away to offer a guest or grandchildren who had come to visit. And, when someone needed a dessert, Mama's homemade strudel was always a big hit.

*****

Strudel

This is my recipe, which is updated and adapted from Mama's.

For the dough:
Two cups of flour
8 ounces sour cream
½ pound sweet butter or margarine
For Filling One:
1 cup finely chopped walnuts or
  almonds

1 cup raisins
1 cup apricot jam or orange
  marmalade
For Filling Two:
½ cup raspberry or strawberry jam
½ cup corn flakes (Mama used Post
  Toasties)

For the Dough:
Mix the butter and cream with a fork. Mix all the ingredients together with a fork to make a soft dough. Add more flour if needed. Roll into 4 balls with your hands. Put dough balls in bowl and cover. Refrigerate at least two hours or overnight. Flour board. Roll out one ball at a time, as thin as possible.

For the Filling:
For Filling One, mix all the ingredients.
For Filling Two, crush the Corn Flakes, mix with the raspberry or strawberry jam. Mix all ingredients together for Filling Two.

Spread Filling One along the rolled out dough about two inches from the bottom. Roll dough over (like a jelly roll) and add a layer of Filling Two, then roll dough again. Continue until end. Be sure to pinch the ends of the roll. Wet top with milk before baking.

Grease pan. Bake at 350 ° for about 30 minutes. Cut while slightly warm into 3/4 inch slices.

For a variation you can use a mixture of cinnamon and sugar (to taste) sprinkled on the dough before adding the fillings. Mama used to add lemon juice and/or rind to Filling Two.

*****

*****

Mandelbrot

2 eggs
¾ cup sugar
½ cup oil or melted sweet butter
2 teaspoons almond extract
2 1/4 cups flour
2 ¼ teaspoons baking powder
1 teaspoon cinnamon
½ cup chopped nuts (almonds or walnuts)

Beat eggs and sugar together. Add oil and almond extract, beat again. Add dry ingredients, then nuts. If you have 2 metal ice trays, grease them. Put ½ mixture in each tray. If you do not have metal ice trays, form the dough into two loaves. Bake in 350° oven for 20 minutes. Cool slightly, then remove from trays. Slice each into about 18 pieces. Place on cookie sheet and brown in 325° oven about 15 minutes, until golden brown in color.

*****

With Esther driving, Mama fussed and sputtered about the traffic and development in Palo Alto and the wider region. When television became available, she became a television news and educational program watcher (especially programs on psychology), and soon graduated to social commentary and criticism, which included giving the family daily updates about the "Respublicans", that man Ike, McCarthyism, and communism. She really enjoyed seeing and hearing Krushchev at the United Nations on TV. "He is speaking Russian," she told us. And, when Sputnik was launched, she worried about the race to space resulting from this, and wondered how the poor would be fed. Mostly, however, she loved her garden and looked forward to visits from her children, grandchildren and neighboring children. Yet life was about to change dramatically for the family.

The first harbinger of change was that, towards the end of the 1950s, Esther became annoyed enough with Mama's increasing demands that she decided to live on her own. The move was amicable once the decision was taken, and Esther moved into a new apartment in downtown Palo Alto which she really enjoyed and where she could walk to work or to shop. She entertained frequently and took great pride in her small deck-garden. Esther happily lived in this suite, well into her 80s, and until she could no longer care for herself.

Esther's 90th Birthday Party Richard, Dorie, Louise, David, Jeanette, Sydney, Esther is sitting

LMC (Levin Metals Corporation)

In the 1950s, the salvage business grew along with the development of California. My three brothers capitalized on this growth opportunity, and (not unlike Papa) used the profits to buy more real estate in and around San Jose. For example, in the late 1950s and early 1960s, all three of my brothers bought recreation property in Boulder Creek, which was a quiet rural community, nestled in the Santa Cruz mountains just west of Los Gatos (see the chapter on the Levin Ranch). Richard also bought a great deal of property, including a cattle ranch and condominiums on Maui in Hawaii.

Richard, ever the visionary, was always for expanding the business, for buying new (and expensive) equipment, and more land. He didn't mind leverage. In fact, one time he leveraged himself so close that the business almost went bankrupt. David was satisfied with a more modest approach to the business, and this difference caused some friction between the brothers. I am certain Syd often found himself as the peacemaker. In the end, David asked Richard to buy him out, and was able to retire with the proceeds and rentals from his real-estate investments by about the time he turned 50. After he retired, David became very active in the San Jose temple. He also enjoyed spending time with his children, grandchildren and, of course, gardening.

Richard and Sydney continued to expand the business from the end of the 1950s through the early 1980s. During this time of growth, Richard and Sydney encouraged other male family members to come and work in the business. For example, Bob Levin (Henry's son) worked for many years for LMC before starting his own recycling business. My nephews Bob Lewon and Joe Smolen also worked for LMC for a number of years—both starting in the yard. Bob, who started with LMC in 1963, left in 1975 to start his own consulting business. At Richard's request he returned in 1983 to serve as president of the company, and stayed on as senior executive for a number of years after the business was sold in 1988. Joe, when he worked for LMC, developed the very successful precious-metals business for the company (extracting gold and silver from used electronic equipment) before leaving to start his own company. Even my son, Stephen worked at LMC for a couple of summers when he was in high school. And Richard, of course, encouraged two of his sons-in-law, Landon George and David Jordan, to work for LMC, which they did for a time before they left the company to start their own enterprises. Thus, it is not surprising that the family management tradition continues. Gary Levin, Syd's son, is now president of the Levin enterprises.

Rubin Lewon, Jeanette's husband, also ended up working at LMC for a number of years. Initially a chemist for an asbestos company, Rubin joined his brothers to develop a salvage business in San Francisco in the 1950's.

In 1961, Rubin's brothers decided to close the business and move back to Salt Lake. Rubin, who loved the outdoors, had no interest in leaving California, especially to move to Utah. Because LMC was continuing to expand, Richard and Sydney offered him the opportunity to buy into LMC. Rubin became the manager responsible for coordinating the machinery retail division of the company, until he decided to retire in 1971. After retiring, Rubin and Jeanette traveled a great deal and the family story about them is that they likely played golf at every course in the United States. Sadly he died from asbestos lung cancer in 1979.

Levin Metals Corporation

The end of the war signaled the beginning of a new era in the Santa Clara Valley. More scrap passed through Levin's International Division than any other individual yard on the West Coast.

As the business grew, Levin Metals Corporation positioned itself to dismantle factories and ships, and, after the Korean War, began to sell used scrap-iron to Japan. This idea rapidly expanded, during the 1960s, into selling a range of metals to Japan, Korea, Taiwan and Australia. By the mid 1960s, LMC had purchased its own fleet of ships to carry the amount of cargo heading to Asia, and also bought a terminal in Richmond to service them. By the 1970s, LMC was considered to be the largest salvage company on the west coast of the United States.

The terminal and the ancillary sites in California were a fantastic asset to the company, and the business grew even more because of the integrated approach LMC had pioneered. There is, however, an interesting postscript to the Richmond terminal. The U.S. Army owned the terminal prior to LMC, and, during the war and just after, disposed of unused or old chemicals, such as DDT, by pouring them on the ground. In those days, nobody except Rachel Carson seemed to be worried about the ecological impacts resulting from such chemicals. By the time the late 1960s came around, and the environmental effects were better understood, the U.S. Government created legislation (the Superfund) to clean up such sites. The Richmond terminal was listed as one of the first sites in the United States for clean-up. This created endless legal grief for LMC, which, although it had not created the pollution, was stuck with the clean-up bill. Unfortunately, the only people who seem to have really cleaned up are the lawyers. And, more than thirty years later, while the legal challenges and counter-challenges were thought to have been finally settled for the Richmond terminal, there still appear to be outstanding legal issues.

In 1979, Richard bought out Sydney, and became the sole owner of LMC until 1988, when he sold most of the business to Sims, an Australian consortium. Sydney was 52 when he retired, and, recognizing the opportunities for growth in the real estate market in California, he invested wisely, both in the Stockton and San Jose areas. He and Virginia traveled as often as they could, until she died in 1995. Syd, however, has always loved the land and, not surprisingly, especially enjoyed his ranch and horses in Boulder Creek. Over the years, he has expanded and landscaped the property, while encouraging the family to come visit. Today, Syd would be called a gentleman cymbidium-orchid farmer, although he and his second wife, Peggy, also ride horses as often as they can. Big Red, of the Hoover Tower fame, is long gone, but Syd has Hercules, a beautiful Tennessee Walker, and this year, for his 80th birthday, told the family he has added a Harley Davidson Hawg!

Shattered Dreams

In the post-World War II / Korean War era, Palo Alto business was booming for Henriques Interiors. As a result, in the 1950s, Fred and I decided to move into a larger family home on Pitman Avenue in Palo Alto. It was a lovely home with a fantastic garden. We were very happy there, and, for our twentieth wedding anniversary, we built a swimming pool in the large back yard instead of taking a trip to Hawaii. At the time, swimming pools were fairly uncommon, so many friends and family came to play by the pool, especially on weekends. We hosted Big Game parties (when the Stanford vs. University of California game was played at the Stanford stadium), and we often had large family dinners for at least one of the Jewish holidays and Thanksgiving. It seemed like our home was Party Central and, believe me, Fred loved a party.

Mama and Esther's Birthday Party, 1958: Back row: Richard, Dorie, Ted, Rubin, Jeanette, Sydney. Center row: Emmy Lou, Louise, Winnie, Mama, Esther, Elaine, Virgina. Front row: Fred, David, Ted Kay

In January, 1959, Fred, who did most of the buying for the store, went on a short buying trip to Oakland. Initially, he wanted me to go with him, but I had a conflict because of a previous arrangement to look at a piece of property. When I got home that afternoon, the Rabbi and a couple of friends were at the house with the children. I couldn't figure out what was going on until they told me that Fred had been killed earlier that day, in an automobile accident. In fact, Fred had been involved in two accidents that day—one on the approach to, and one on, the San Mateo Bridge, less than a mile apart from each other. The first accident was a result of another driver stopping unexpectedly in the middle of the highway, and Fred's car being hit by a third car hitting the first car. He was not badly injured, but his car caught fire, and he was taken to the hospital. He called our store manager, Ed Johnson, to come and pick him up from hospital. Coming home, a drunk driver, passing on the wrong side of the two-lane road, ran head-on into the car. Fred was killed instantly, and Ed was severely injured, although he eventually recovered after a long struggle.

The whole family and the community were in shock. It was a huge news item in the local press because Fred was so well known in the area, and the accident also was reported across the country, because of the strangeness of the events. The funeral was held at Roller and Hapgood Funeral Parlor (Beth Am was yet to be built), and was so large—it seemed that everybody who had worked with Fred, or was taught by him, wanted to come—that they had to put loudspeakers outside to accommodate all the people who came to the service. I remember very little about the funeral, and the months following, because I was in such severe shock. I do remember, however, that about six months after Fred's death, I received a letter from an overzealous civil servant and a bill from the state, for damage to the bridge. Fortunately, Gerry Marcus, who by this time was a senior partner in a large San Francisco law firm, and counselor for the Levin family, resolved this error.

Not surprisingly, after the shock wore off, I became very depressed, but I tried, with Esther's help, to keep the business going. We had excellent decorators to help in the store, but Fred was the business. Plus, I was so uncertain that every time somebody said the store looked different, I was convinced it was a criticism. Thus, in September of 1959, nine months after Fred died, I sold the business, and tried to get on with my life and find a way to bring happiness once again into the lives of my children.

The 1960s

Recognizing that I needed to support my family, and that a woman over 35 years old was not in high demand, I went to see a financial planner to help me sort out my options. For example, I knew I didn't have any decorating talent, and I knew I didn't want to go back to banking at a meager salary, but I didn't know what I wanted to do. Initially, I had thought of going into real estate, but I also knew that I wanted to be home on weekends, rather than away from my family, so I was quite confused. Not knowing what to expect, I was surprised at the outcome of the meeting, because, at the end of the interview, the person who was interviewing me immediately offered me a job with his company, selling mutual funds and life insurance. Subsequently, the firm sent me to San Francisco to take a battery of tests to confirm my skills.

Because I was still so uncertain about myself, and my skills, my sister Elaine suggested that I call our cousin Joe Edelstein, who was a broker with York and Company, to ask him about the firm offering me a job. I called on Joe, who introduced me to Mr. York, and, the next day, I was offered a job to become a stockbroker. I immediately accepted. After being trained for six months, I received my brokerage license by mid-year in 1960, and started working. I didn't know it at the time, but I was one of the first female brokers on the west coast. Eventually, I joined J. Barth and Company, which became Dean Witter, and worked out of the Menlo Park office until I retired in 1974. I have to say that, when I started, there were few opportunities for female brokers, but, with hard work, I not only survived, but did very well, in spite of the obstacles. Today, I am happy to say, it is a different story for women brokers who have the desire and skills to be successful in the business.

As for the rest of the family, it was growing again. The three oldest grandchildren—Stanley, Alan and Joan—all had married, and were now bringing great grandchildren to visit Mama. The rest of the grandchildren seemed as if they all became teenagers at the same time, graduated college, one after another, and, toward the end of the 1960s, many married their college sweethearts. Esther continued working for the new owners of Henriques Interiors and while she could never bring herself to drive to see Jackie (her son), who was living in a care facility in Sonoma County,

Dorie, and Bob Lewon and his wife, Elaine, would frequently take her to see him. When my sister Elaine divorced her third husband, Ted Kay, and subsequently moved to Palm Springs, she met and married Homer Cobb, saying that she finally had found happiness. Sadly, she became the third family member to die of bowel cancer, in 1973.

Mama continued her social commentary well into the 1960s, but it was now about different kinds of issues—the injustices in the United States to people of color, the poor in Appalachia and the race riots. She watched the events surrounding the civil rights marches with a keen interest, saying, "If they can discriminate against the coloreds, we are next." The 1963 march on Washington was a big event for Mama and she told us that "Freedom is for all of us."

Mama could never resist a dance

Mama Gets Sick

In 1965, when Mama was 82, she suffered from some mysterious physical ailment. We never knew exactly what it was, except that she cried out, in the middle of the night, that something was happening to her head. Cedolia (the housekeeper who stayed with Mama) called me, and I rushed Mama to the hospital. The doctors conducted a series of tests and said she had some kind of stroke, but there was little they could do for her. That was really the beginning of the end.

On behalf of the family I hired a wonderful woman, Marie Harris, to look after Mama when she was finally able to come home. Marie came in every other day for 24 hours and another woman from San Jose took the other shift. On the weekends one of us usually stayed with Mama. Esther often volunteered and went out of her way to try and help. As a family, we were committed to trying to keep Mama in her home as long as possible and to ensuring that we did not leave her. Marie was extremely patient, making Mama as comfortable as possible, and trying re-establish old routines—even encouraging Mama to cook family favorites, to keep her mind active. However, when the second nurse left, we had a difficult time finding proper help. Moreover, it was evident that Mama was never going to recover, and, in fact, that she was no longer able to care for herself and was getting worse.

One evening, one of Mama's neighbors called me to complain about the noise he heard each night at the house. I rushed over, and found that Mama was tied in her bed, and was yelling for help and trying to get up. Cedolia and the hired nurse were in the living room, watching television with the sound turned to full volume. Obviously, it was time to make the difficult decision about what to do with Mama. After much family debate, we decided to put Mama in an extended-care facility (it was called a "rest home") in Sunnyvale. Mama hated it and let everyone know it. She yelled, swore loudly (something she had never done), and called all the nurses really obscene names. Sydney, who went to see her the day after she was moved, remembers that Mama was furious with everyone and everything at the rest home, and let everyone know it in full voice. Syd quieted her, and told her that she was not being polite, and that seemed to work, because the yelling and name calling stopped.

Julia Levin dies, Jewish leader

Julia Levin, 90, a leader in the Peninsula Jewish community for decades, died Monday at a Sunnyvale convalescent home, after a long illness.

K n o w n affectionately as "Mama Levin," the native of Russia was one of the founders of Congregation Beth Jacob, now in Redwood City. The once-tiny congregation first met for services in 1933, in the Palo Alto home of Mrs. Levin and her late husband, Jacob. Later, the congregation outgrew a small building in Menlo Park, and built its present synagogue on Alameda de las Pulgas, Redwood City, in the mid-1950s.

Mrs. Levin came to the United States after the turn of the century and settled in Palo Alto in 1905. Her home was at 2329 Cowper St.

The first president of the Sisterhood of Congregation Beth Jacob, Mrs. Levin also was a founder of the Peninsula Chapter of Hadassah, an international Jewish women's service league.

Friends remember Mama Levin as an expansive person. "I love everyone," she was fond of saying, one recalled.

S u r v i v o r s include four daughters, Mrs. Esther Jacobson of Palo Alto, Mrs. Louise Henriques of Menlo Park, Mrs. Dorie Smolen of San Mateo, and Mrs. Rubin Lewon of Los Gatos; three sons, David, Richard and Sydney Levin, all of San Jose; a brother, Sam Edelstein of Redwood City; 17 grandchildren and 25 great-grandchildren.

Funeral services were held today (at 3 p.m.) at the Oak Hill Mortuary's Chapel of the Roses, 300 Curtner Ave., San Jose, with Rabbi Joseph Gitin, of Temple Emanu-El, San Jose, and Rabbi Herbert D. Teitelbaum, of Temple Beth Jacob, officiating. Burial was at the Home of Peace Cemetery, San Jose.

The family prefers memorials be contributions to a favorite charity.

Julia's obituary Palo Alto Historical Association

In any event, after Mama's initial episodes, the doctors kept her heavily sedated to keep her calm.

Mama was at the rest home until she died, in 1974. Because all of us were concerned that Mama not feel deserted, we asked Marie Harris to be with her during the week. During the first few years, Marie would take Mama to visit Esther for luncheon on a weekly basis. As Mama became more arthritic, and was confined to a wheelchair, Marie would take her out for daily walks to see the blue sky and flowers, because it gave her such pleasure. Of course, on the weekends, all we kids and the grandchildren came to visit. To the end, she always knew everybody's name, even though the doctors said she remembered little.

In her last years, Mama disappeared behind an old and sick shell, which was a sad end to a vibrant life. Mama was a great lady, a loving and caring person who was always there for us. She was kind, steadfast, and the creative entrepreneur in our family. Papa, who was respected widely, would not have been as successful without her. Together, my parents, along with our extended family, raised us and sustained us in good times, and in tough times. They never let us down. I'd like to think that our family is what it is because of the vision they brought with them to America of a better world. Our job is to keep the vision bright, and live it in our daily lives.

This is not the right note on which to leave the Levin family story. There is the old saying "A family that plays together, stays together." It is certainly true for the extended Levin mishpucah, and, whether as children or as adults, our extended family has always looked forward to being together for the holidays and other celebrations.

Our family has always have enjoyed just spending time together—and telling stories. My surviving brother, Syd, and sister, Dorie, and I speak to each other several times a

The Meshugge Mishpucah, 1978.
Back Row: Milton Mann, Ted Smolen, David Levin, Richard Levin, Esther Jacobson.
Middle: Dorie Smolen, Emmy Lou Levin, Winnie Levin, Syd Levin.
Front: Louise Henriques Mann, Jeanette Lewon, Rulein Lewon, Donna Levin, Stan Levin

week, and we try and see each other as much as possible. Likewise, Gerry and Elie Marcus, have been an important part of my life, that of my brothers, and of my children and grandchildren. The grandchildren (the cousins), and great grandchildren don't live geographically as close to each other as my generation, but they use e-mail to keep in touch, and visit with each other as much as possible.

In 2002, some of my immediate family (three generations, in fact) celebrated Passover at the home of my nephew Stan and his wife, Donna. And it was a celebration—one which, for me, captured everything about our family which I learned to love and admire as a child, and which is alive and well today. Some things have changed. In the new millennium, both the women and men contribute to the Seder.

Gerry and Ellis Marcus, with Louise (at my 80th birthday party)

The gefilte fish may be out of a bottle, but the matzoh balls are always homemade and superb. The tradition of laughter and jokes has stayed the same, but the wine has sure improved. The kids are always late to the table—this past year, my granddaughter and her friends were almost two hours late driving from San Francisco, and my grandson had to call for a rescue to help find his car keys at the local ski-hill. Our family has become more diverse: it now transcends race and faith, but the tradition of pre-dinner prayers and not much post-dinner religion continues. For our family, for our children and grandchildren, it works. We are blessed because we have inherited the gift of love.

Epilogue

Just in case you didn't notice . . . In passing on the story of our family, there are several reminders from Mama and Papa that I want to leave with my children and grandchildren. I hope you remember them.

My life has spanned the 20th century—from horse and wagon, to spaceships; from newspapers, to the radio, to the TV, to the Internet. In fact, if there has been a constant theme to my life, it is that everything changes. One can only wonder what changes will happen in the 21st century. Thus, in this time of constant change, the challenge for the younger generation is to appreciate where you come from; to learn from and have pride in your family's history; to remember that nobody said life is easy; to work hard to make your own luck; and to understand that we often find the best in ourselves through hard work and service to mankind. Oh, and as Mama used to say, "Don't worry! It doesn't do any good."

Family is important. In the early days, there was a real closeness among all of the family. Family meant so much to us on a day-to-day basis because, being Jewish, we were, in many ways, isolated from the larger community. We were a separate solitude from the larger community. Today, this is not the case, which makes it even more important to take the time to celebrate family. For example, Mama and Papa taught us that simple things like mealtimes are important, because it is a time that the family gathers together, as are other family events or religious rituals. Make the time to enjoy them.

Things aren't that important. While it is a blessing to be comfortable and have what you need, as children we knew we were loved, and were happy with simple, handmade toys, and one drawer in a dresser. My parents taught us to focus on what we had—not what we didn't have. Kindness to each other and to strangers was honored. Materialism isn't the answer to kindness, or to giving and receiving love.

Nor is wealth an end in itself. Mama taught us to use our wealth to help others less fortunate.

Take care of yourself. There is a history of breast and bowel cancer in our family. However, don't be afraid. I am a breast-cancer survivor because I paid attention. Also, there may be a hereditary depression gene that runs in the family. Doctors say that this type of depression can be fixed if treated early. If you don't feel well, go see the doctor—sooner, rather than later. As the doctors in the family say, your genetic endowment is part of your history, so pay attention to your body and your mind. Or, as others in the family say, "Use it, or lose it" applies to your mind as well as other parts of your body.

Finally, our family has adapted and changed over the last century, but, keeping your word, telling the truth, and practicing the Golden Rule of "Do unto others as you would have them do unto you," are the core values of our family and they do not change with the times. While circumstances may change, you are always responsible for your behavior, and, as Papa always said, "When you die, all you can leave is a good or bad name."

So remember this: Learn from the past, enjoy today and look forward to the future!

Appendix

Perhaps it is just as well that we cannot trace our ancestors too far back in time: Those whom we have been able to record have done more than enough to confuse us. We don't just have a family tree, we have a forest!

The diagram of "The Mishpucah" found in this appendix is not a true family tree. Let it be considered a collection of "cousins". It is also not accurate in other respects. *Papa Barkusky* and *Lustenick Older Sister* are people whose names are unknown to us. Thus, it was necessary to "invent them" to graph out the relationships.

There are several other unusual features, including:

Joseph Edelstein, who married many times, was first married to the older Lustenick sister. After her death, he married Esther Lustenick (1), a younger sister who was the widow of Isidor Dickenfadden. Esther and Isidor were the parents of Julia Dickenfadden Levin. Thus, Esther appears in two locations on the tree: as mother of Julia, and also as mother of Jack, Nathan and Sam Edelstein. This union created cousins being stepbrothers/sisters, and must have created confusion for the immigration officials at Ellis Island. It also created a nightmare for graphing the family tree.

In the next generation, Dora Levin (2) married Sam Edelstein, a half brother to Julia Levin. Thus, Dora appears as a child of Ellis and Anne Levin, as well as on the Edelstein side, as wife of Sam.

The Family Tree is current to January 2003 — more or less. Some cousins have requested that we not include their ex-spouses where no children were produced. We also have not included "significant others". As well, we made no distinction between natural children and stepchildren, if they are currently living with one of the mishpucah. It appears this is the family tradition, and extends back as far as we have records. Further, change is constant. Three members of our family have died since we printed the family tree—cousins Audre Marcus, Harold Edelstein, and my sister-in-law, Emmy Lou Levin.

The mechanics of the tree were daunting. The software program we used for graphing makes no distinction between males and females, except that the males have double lines around the boxes and the females have single lines. Also, we tried to establish maternal lineage as per our Jewish roots, but alas, the software doesn't seem to accept such designation. Rather, lineage is arbitrary, according to what best fits on an 8x12 page.

Obviously, we have not been able to achieve 100% accuracy with this endeavor. Consider this an ongoing experiment. Additions and corrections are welcome.

The Mishpucah

Edelstein-Barrish Branch

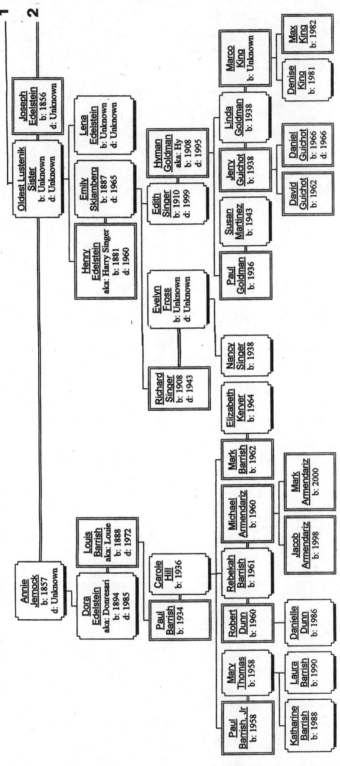

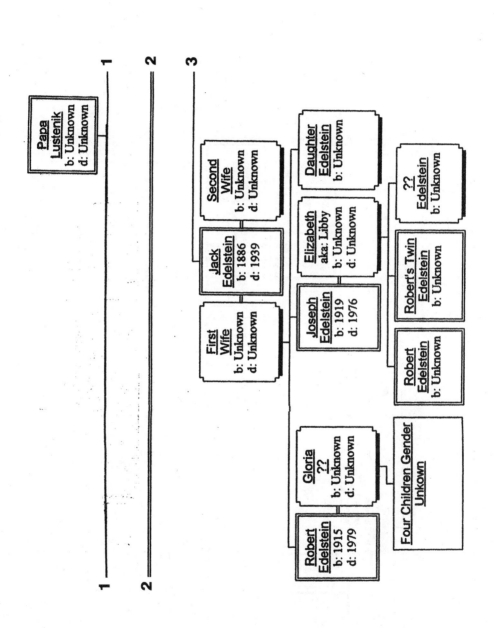

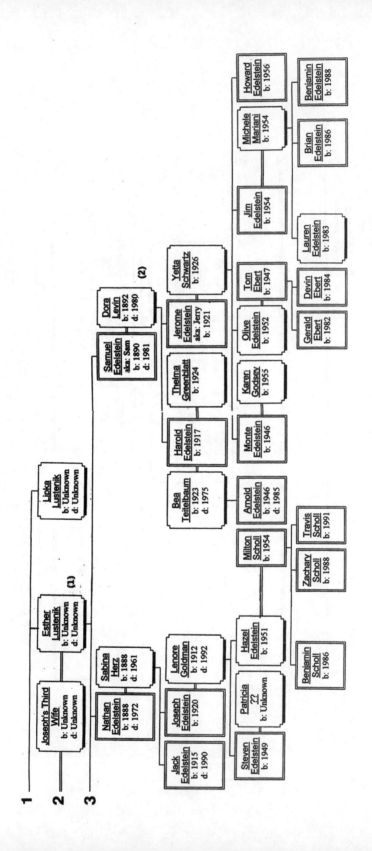

Ellis and Anne Levin Branch

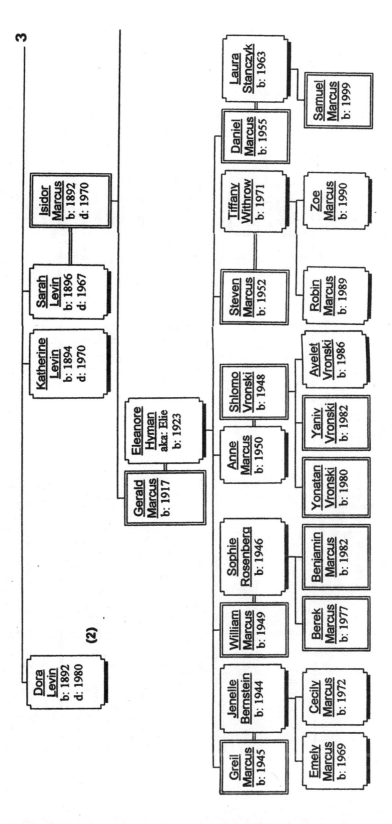

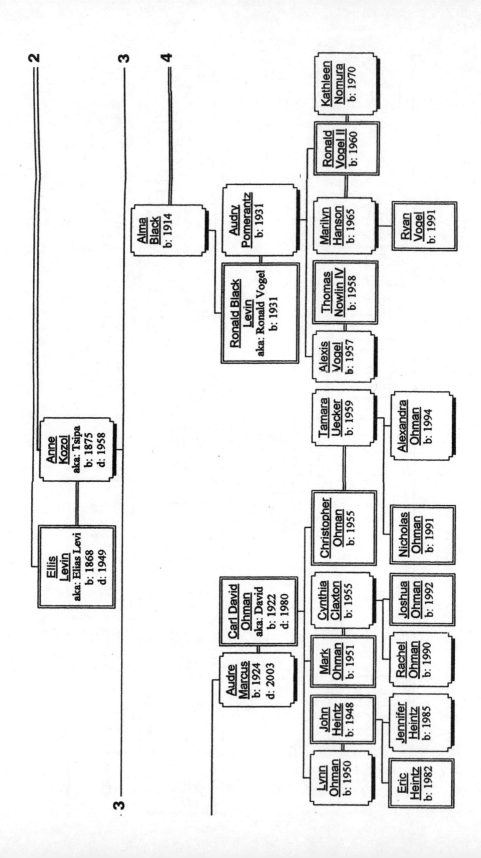

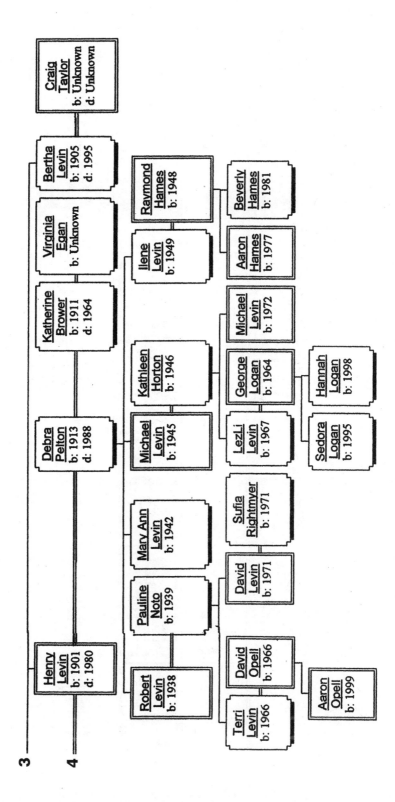

Jacob and Julia Levin Branch

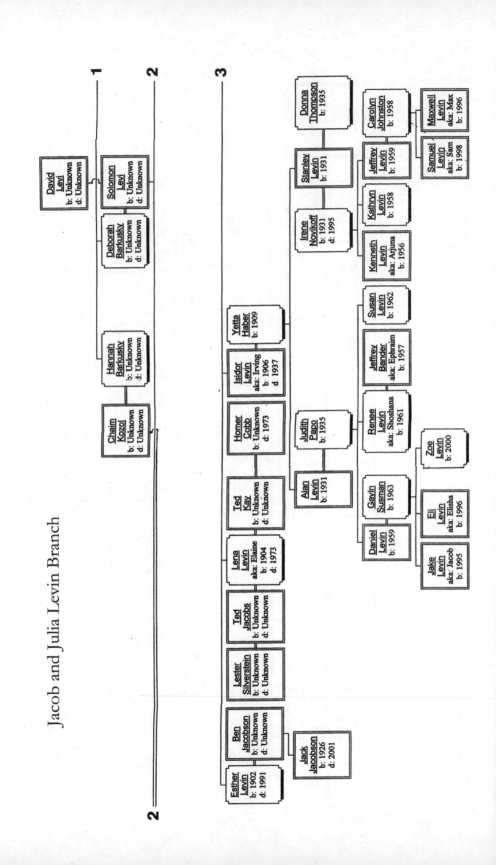

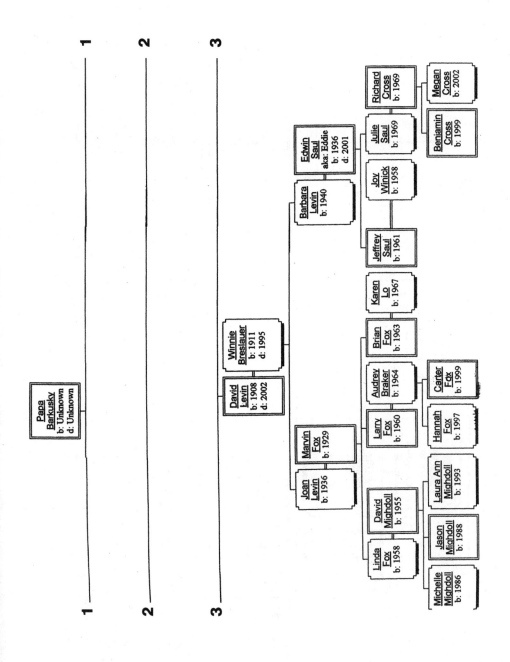

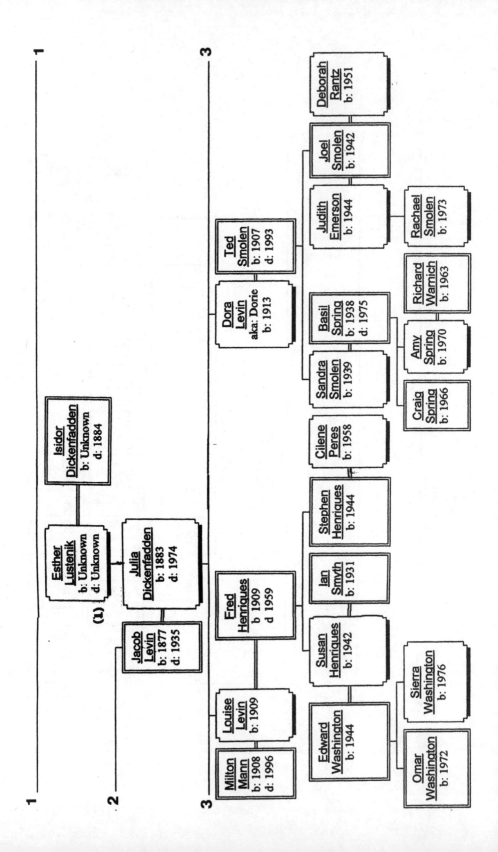

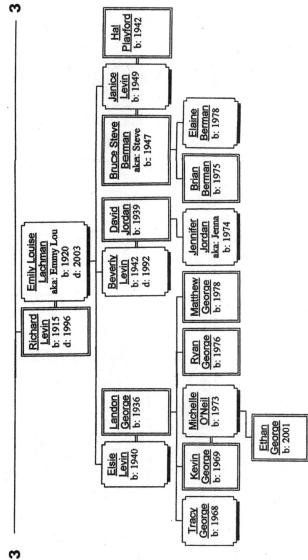

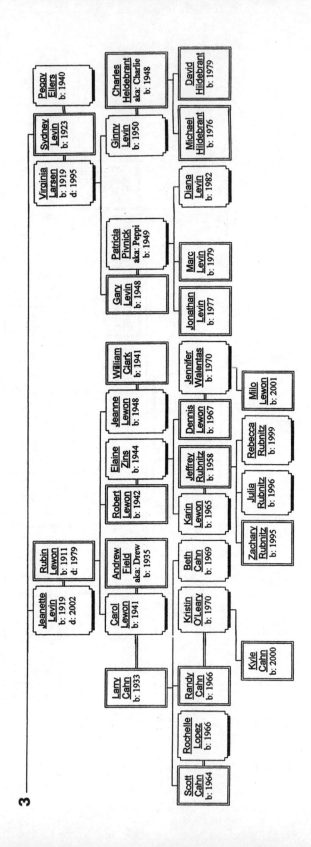

Barkusky-Barrish Branch

- **Feive Barkusky** — b: Unknown, d: Unknown
  - **Louis Barrish** (aka: Louie) — b: 1888, d: 1972 & **Pauline Barkus** — b: 1893, d: 1923
    - **Samuel** — b: Unknown, d: Unknown
    - **Ruth Barrish** — b: 1920, d: 1960 & **Lewis Actor** — b: 1917
      - **Patrice** — b: Unknown, d: Unknown
        - **Jack Barrish** — b: 1916, d: 1999 & **Kay Johnson** — b: 1906, d: 1985
      - **Phil Actor** — b: 1944 & **Lynn Kirby** — b: 1951
        - **Alexis Actor** — b: 1973
        - **Armondo Sanchez** — b: 1973
          - **Aron Sanchez** — b: 1996
          - **Anabel Sanchez** — b: 2002
        - **Andrea Actor** — b: 1978
          - **Grayson Actor** — b: 1998
      - **David Actor** — b: 1949 & **Lisa Trimble** — b: 1957
        - **Daniel Actor** — b: 1989
        - **Charles Actor** — b: 1992
      - **Judith Actor** (aka: Judy) — b: 1949, d: 2000 & **Alan Pendley** — b: 1948
        - **Jason Pendley** — b: 1975
        - **Marla Pendley** — b: 1979

- **Gary Actor** — b: 1944 & **Diana Milam** — b: 1947
  - **James Actor** — b: 1967 & **Rebecca Redding** — b: 1970
  - **Ruth Actor** — b: 1969 & **Mark Gomez** — b: 1969, d: 2000
    - **Christopher Gomez** — b: 1989
    - **Marcus Gomez** — b: 1991
  - **Andreas Sanchez** — b: 1993